PLACES AND CASES
The UK

Peter Webber

Series Editor
Peter Webber

Stanley Thornes (Publishers) Ltd

First published in 1998 by:
Stanley Thornes (Publishers) Ltd
Ellenborough House
Wellington Street
CHELTENHAM GL50 1YW
England

98 99 00 01 02 / 10 9 8 7 6 5 4 3 2 1

A catalogue record for this book is available from the British Library.

ISBN 0-7487-2915-1

Printed and bound in Italy by STIGE, Turin

Acknowledgements

With thanks to the following for permission to reproduce photographs and other copyright material in this book:

Aerofilms, 86 (Fig. E); Anglesey Aluminium Metal Ltd, 57; Associated British Ports, 94 (Fig. C); Birmingham City Council, 78; BP/Sillson Communications, 20 (Fig. B); Sylivia Cordaiy, 23; Country Commission/Peter Hamilton, 24; Department of Agriculture for Northern Ireland Rural Development, 92, 93; English Nature, 35 (Fig. D); Environment Agency, 33; The *Guardian*/Don McPhee, 29 (Fig. D); Honda of the UK Manufacturing Ltd, 60, 61; ICI Chemical and Polymers PLC, 35 (Fig. C), 54; Kitchenham Ltd, 20 (Fig. A); Meadowhall Centre Ltd, 89; Northumbrian Water/Kingham Davies, 36; NRSC Air Photo Group, 37; Science Photo Library 4, 14; Sheffield City Council/Andy Barker 39, 86 (Figs F, G, H); Sheffield City Council, Development, Environment, Leisure and Planning, 85; Skyscan, 75; Still Pictures, 34, 39; Swansea Centre for Trade and Industry, 64; Trip Photographic Library, 56; University of Dundee Satellite Receiving Station, 13; Vickers Properties Development, 59, 76; Simon Warner, 29 (Fig. E); Welsh Development Agency, 67; Westminster Dredging Co. Ltd, 19.

All other photos by Daniel Webber, David Webber and the author.

AA Publishing for the road atlas map extract, Fig. A, page 70; Council for the Protection of Rural England, Fig. B, page 25; Countryside Commission, for material from *Countryside*, Issue 3 (January/February 1996), Fig. A, page 24; *The Economist*, Fig. D, page 47; Northern Ireland Dept of Agriculture © Crown copyright, Fig. F, page 93; Maps reproduced from the Ordnance Survey Landranger mapping with the permission of The Controller of Her Majesty's Stationery Office © Crown copyright, Licence Number 07000U, Fig. A, page 9, Fig. C, page 21, Fig. B, page 34, Fig. C, page 41, Fig. I, page 67, Fig. A, page 82; *The Times*, Fig. F, page 29; Yorkshire Water, Fig. C, page 28.

Every effort has been made to contact copyright holders. The publishers apologise to anyone whose rights have been inadvertently overlooked, and will be happy to rectify any errors or omissions.

Contents

Introduction

To the student

This book about the UK is one in a series of three textbooks for GCSE Geography. Book One covers Europe, while a third looks at worldwide issues.

You will find that much of the book consists of case studies. There is some background information about a topic before many of the case studies are introduced. For example, the case study on page 28 looks at Yorkshire Water. Before the case study, the materials get you to think about renewable and non-renewable resources and their management, and about rivers and drainage basins. However, if you are able to make the best of the case study, you need to have ideas already about the sources of water and their management. This is why there is a 'Do you know?' box in each unit. It is assumed that you use a 'core' geography textbook and will have some class time to make sure you know the definitions and the answers to any questions in the 'Do you know?' box before you study the topics in this book. This case study approach allows you to deepen and broaden your knowledge and understanding.

The case studies have been chosen to cover the main topics you need for your GCSE syllabuses. So you will find case studies on landforms, ecosystems, weather and climate, population, settlement, development and environmental issues. Most GCSE examinations either include case studies for you to analyse, or ask you to use a case study you have studied. This book, therefore, gives you practice and examples. You will find that the activities throughout the book will help you develop the different skills you need in examinations. These include using photographs, tables, graphs, maps, diagrams, charts, as well as reading sections of text and completing decision making exercises. This book gives you plenty of practice!

The symbol ➤ suggests that you write at greater length and in more detail. Your answer should be at least a paragraph in length.

Some of the words which appear in bold throughout this book are key terms which are defined in the Glossary on page 96.

Geography is all about how the world works – the natural world and the human world – and is about more than examinations. So, we hope this book will help you to take an interest in and begin to understand the world around you.

Enjoy your Geography!

Figure A: Satellite image of the British Isles

UK	1961	1971	1981	1985	1994
Population (thousands)	52,807	55,907	56,379	56,845	58,395
Birth rate (per thousand)	17.9	16.2	13.2	13.2	14.0
Death rate (per thousand)	12.0	11.5	11.7	11.8	11.0
Natural increase	5.9	4.7	1.5	1.4	3.0
Infant mortality (per thousand)	22.1	18.0	11.2	9.4	6.0
Life expectancy (years)					
males	67.9	68.8	69.8	71.4	73.0
females	73.8	75.0	76.2	77.2	79.0

Figure B: Population change in the United Kingdom

Migration into and out of the UK (thousands)				
	1971	1981	1985	1994
immigration	199.7	153	270	253
emigration	240	233	174	191
net migration	−40.3	−80	+96	+62

Figure C: Migration in the UK

The political and regional background

The map shows the British Isles which comprises England, Scotland, Wales and Northern Ireland which make up the United Kingdom, and the Republic of Ireland (Eire). They lie between latitudes 50°N and 61°N.

A **region** is identified by having features or characteristics in common. These features may be physical, economic or social.

The economic regions are just one of the many types of region within the United Kingdom. They overlap with other regions such as those used by the British government for granting regional assistance e.g. Development Areas and Intermediate areas. The European Union has different criteria for defining regions such as industrial regions in decline or rural areas. The location of the case studies relating to regions are indicated on the map.

**Figure D:
Swindon town centre**

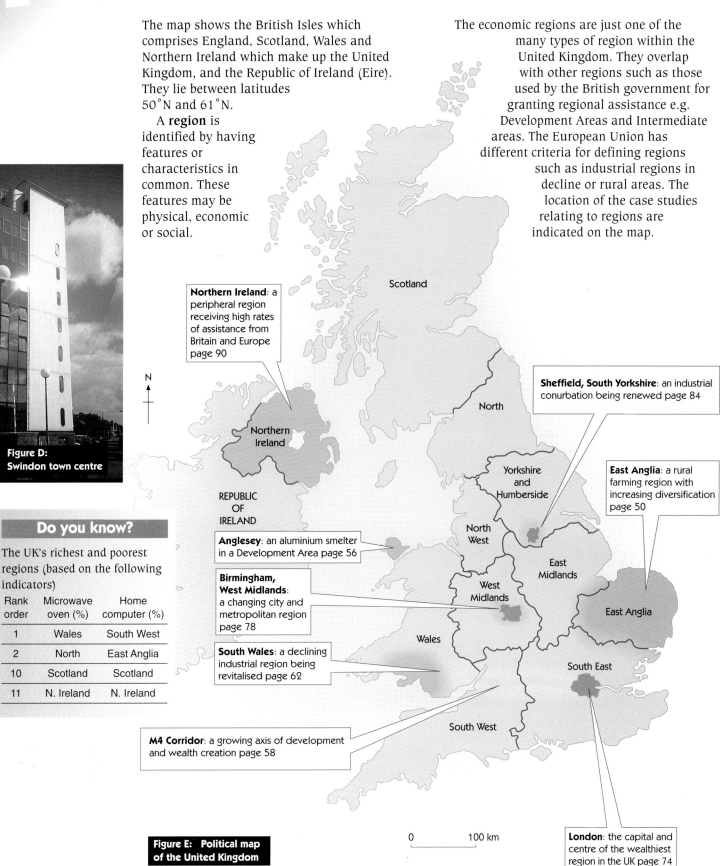

Northern Ireland: a peripheral region receiving high rates of assistance from Britain and Europe page 90

Sheffield, South Yorkshire: an industrial conurbation being renewed page 84

East Anglia: a rural farming region with increasing diversification page 50

Anglesey: an aluminium smelter in a Development Area page 56

Birmingham, West Midlands: a changing city and metropolitan region page 78

South Wales: a declining industrial region being revitalised page 62

M4 Corridor: a growing axis of development and wealth creation page 58

London: the capital and centre of the wealthiest region in the UK page 74

Scotland

North

Yorkshire and Humberside

North West

East Midlands

West Midlands

East Anglia

Wales

South East

South West

Northern Ireland

REPUBLIC OF IRELAND

N

0   100 km

Figure E: Political map of the United Kingdom

Climate and water supply

The annual rainfall map is linked to the water supply map. The north and west of Britain and Ireland are wetter than the south and east. A high proportion of the population lives in England, and the central areas of England are not self-sufficient in water. Some water is moved from the areas with a surplus to those with a deficit by rivers and pipeline. Some new water transfers are proposed. With droughts becoming more common and the demand for water rising, water supply is set to become a major issue in Britain.

The country's climate does seem to be changing and the climate change map looks ahead to 2050. Unless the demand for water can be substantially reduced then the water supply problem will worsen.

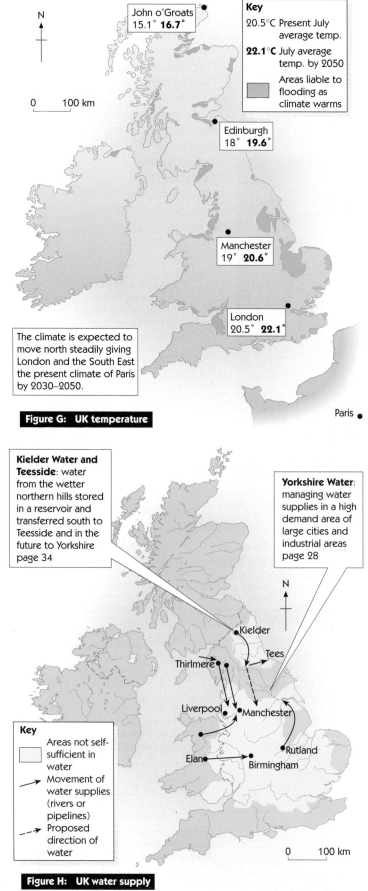

Key
20.5°C Present July average temp.

22.1°C July average temp. by 2050

Areas liable to flooding as climate warms

John o'Groats 15.1° **16.7°**

Edinburgh 18° **19.6°**

Manchester 19° **20.6°**

London 20.5° **22.1°**

The climate is expected to move north steadily giving London and the South East the present climate of Paris by 2030–2050.

Paris

Figure G: UK temperature

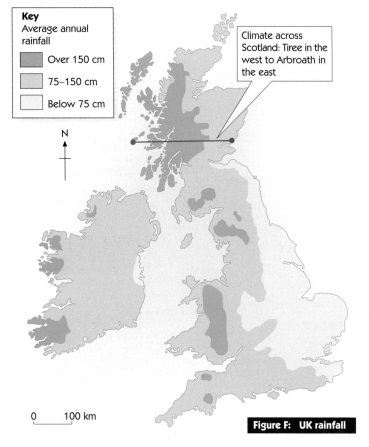

Key
Average annual rainfall

Over 150 cm

75–150 cm

Below 75 cm

Climate across Scotland: Tiree in the west to Arbroath in the east

Figure F: UK rainfall

Kielder Water and Teesside: water from the wetter northern hills stored in a reservoir and transferred south to Teesside and in the future to Yorkshire page 34

Yorkshire Water: managing water supplies in a high demand area of large cities and industrial areas page 28

Kielder

Tees

Thirlmere

Liverpool

Manchester

Elan

Rutland

Birmingham

Key
Areas not self-sufficient in water

→ Movement of water supplies (rivers or pipelines)

⇢ Proposed direction of water

Figure H: UK water supply

Do you know?

? The four climate regions of the British Isles are determined by rainfall figures, and temperatures along isotherms January 5°C and July 15°C.
- NW Britain
- NE Britain
- SW Britain
- SE Britain

The physical and geological background

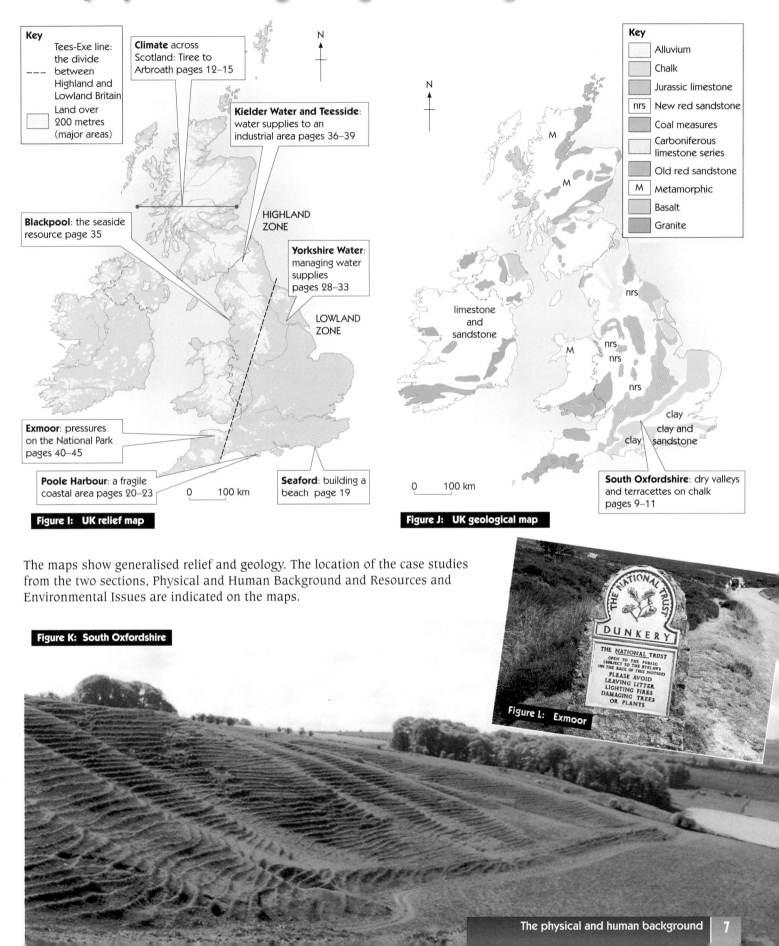

Key

Tees-Exe line: the divide between Highland and Lowland Britain

---

Land over 200 metres (major areas)

Climate across Scotland: Tiree to Arbroath pages 12–15

Kielder Water and Teesside: water supplies to an industrial area pages 36–39

Blackpool: the seaside resource page 35

HIGHLAND ZONE

Yorkshire Water: managing water supplies pages 28–33

LOWLAND ZONE

Exmoor: pressures on the National Park pages 40–45

Poole Harbour: a fragile coastal area pages 20–23

0   100 km

Seaford: building a beach page 19

Figure I: UK relief map

Key

Alluvium

Chalk

Jurassic limestone

nrs   New red sandstone

Coal measures

Carboniferous limestone series

Old red sandstone

M   Metamorphic

Basalt

Granite

limestone and sandstone

nrs

nrs
nrs

nrs

clay

clay and sandstone

clay

0   100 km

South Oxfordshire: dry valleys and terracettes on chalk pages 9–11

Figure J: UK geological map

The maps show generalised relief and geology. The location of the case studies from the two sections, Physical and Human Background and Resources and Environmental Issues are indicated on the maps.

Figure K: South Oxfordshire

THE NATIONAL TRUST

DUNKERY

THE NATIONAL TRUST
OPEN TO THE PUBLIC
(SUBJECT TO THE BYELAWS
ON THE BACK OF THIS NOTICE)
PLEASE AVOID
LEAVING LITTER
LIGHTING FIRES
DAMAGING TREES
OR PLANTS

Figure L: Exmoor

Population distribution and change

The two maps show the varying population densities of the United Kingdom and the changes in population between the censuses of 1981 and 1991. The location of the case studies relating to the section Population and Settlement are indicated on the maps.

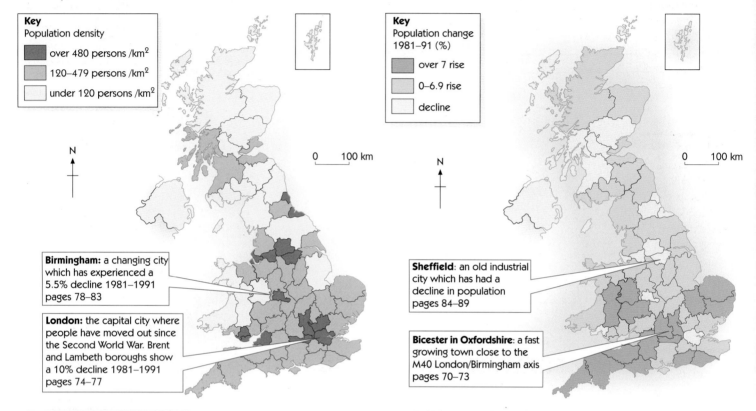

Key
Population density

- over 480 persons /km^2
- 120–479 persons /km^2
- under 120 persons /km^2

N

0   100 km

Birmingham: a changing city which has experienced a 5.5% decline 1981–1991 pages 78–83

London: the capital city where people have moved out since the Second World War. Brent and Lambeth boroughs show a 10% decline 1981–1991 pages 74–77

Figure M: UK population density

Key
Population change 1981–91 (%)

- over 7 rise
- 0–6.9 rise
- decline

N

0   100 km

Sheffield: an old industrial city which has had a decline in population pages 84–89

Bicester in Oxfordshire: a fast growing town close to the M40 London/Birmingham axis pages 70–73

Figure N: Population distribution

The map showing population density reflects the long history of economic development. During the Industrial Revolution, areas of dense population grew up based on the coalfields and heavy industry e.g. Liverpool, Manchester, South Wales and the West Midlands.

The map showing population change reflects two long-established migration processes.

1 The north to south drift of population from the old industrial regions to growing economic areas of southern England.

2 The urban to rural shift from the large conurbations including London.

The areas with the highest **natural increase** are in central southern England, because here there is a higher proportion of younger people.

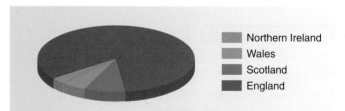

Northern Ireland
Wales
Scotland
England

Population by country (mid-1990s estimates)	
England	48,533,000
Scotland	5,120,000
Wales	2,906,000
Northern Ireland	1,632,000
Total United Kingdom	58,191,000

Figure O: Population by country

Do you know?

? The UK's most densely populated and fastest changing regions

Rank order	Population density	1981–1991 (% change)
1	North West	+ E. Anglia
2	South East	+ S. West
10	N. Ireland	– N. West
11	Scotland	– Scotland

Rocks and landforms

Main activities

This is as OS map interpretation exercise with opportunities for drawing a cross-section and analysing information about chalk landscapes.

Key ideas

● The permeability of chalk make its landforms distinctive.
● There are several theories for the formation of dry valleys.

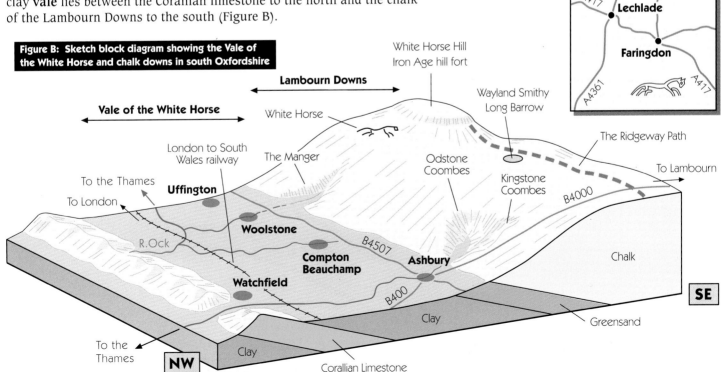

Figure A: Map of the chalk area in South Oxfordshire

© Crown copyright

The Ordnance Survey map extract (Figure A) covers the area of chalk north of Lambourn. The Vale of the White Horse is in south Oxfordshire. The clay **vale** lies between the Corallian limestone to the north and the chalk of the Lambourn Downs to the south (Figure B).

Figure B: Sketch block diagram showing the Vale of the White Horse and chalk downs in south Oxfordshire

Chalk is a **permeable** rock which means water can pass through it and be stored in it. The areas between the particles of chalk are called **pore spaces**. These are larger than in some rocks and water is able to pass down between them. When all the pore spaces are filled with water, the rock becomes saturated. The **water table** is the boundary between the saturated rock and the unsaturated rock above (Figure C). Clay is an **impermeable** rock and does not allow water to pass through it very quickly. The particles of clay are much smaller than those of chalk. Water clings to the grains preventing it from moving through the rock.

A distinctive feature of chalk scenery in England is the **cuesta**. This consists of an **escarpment** (scarp slope) and a **dip slope**. The sedimentary rock was laid down in horizontal layers, but some 35 million years ago it was tilted by earth movements when the African and Eurasian plates collided. The chalk scenery has typical features as shown on the cross-section (Figure C) drawn from the Ordnance Survey map. The approximate geological boundaries and the level of the water table have been sketched in.

Figure D shows that chalk is not a very hard rock; because of its softness it forms gently rounded hills called **downs**. The clay which was laid down before the chalk (and is under the chalk) is a very soft rock and erodes to form **vales**. It is at the edge of the vale where the clay meets the chalk that over a thousand years ago the Anglo-Saxon settlers chose to site their villages. The sketch map (Figure E) shows Woolstone village near to a spring and a small stream. The village is at the foot of the scarp slope near the greensand rock outcrop where it is sheltered and where soil has been brought down the slope. The villagers were able to farm the soils of the chalk and clay. Local wood was used for building and for fuel. Many villages were established at the foot of escarpments and are known as **springline villages**; Compton Beauchamp and Ashbury are other examples on the Ordnance Survey map (Figure A).

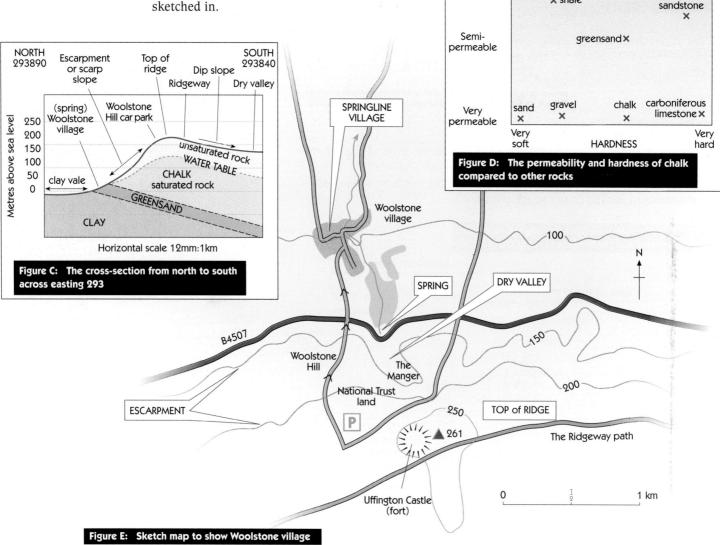

Figure C: The cross-section from north to south across easting 293

Figure D: The permeability and hardness of chalk compared to other rocks

Figure E: Sketch map to show Woolstone village

There are few rivers or streams on chalk landscapes but there are many dry valleys, often called **coombes** in this area. There are several theories about the formation of dry valleys.

1 During the Ice Age, water would have frozen in the pore spaces turning the chalk into impermeable rock. Any surface water, such as summer meltwater, would erode the chalk to form valleys. These conditions are called **periglacial**.

2 Since the Ice Age, the climate has at some times been very much wetter than at others. At wet times the water table rises and normal river erosion can take place.

3 Chalk was once covered by an impermeable rock which had river erosion on it. As the impermeable rock eroded away so the river valleys came through to the chalk (superimposed on the chalk).

4 Sea levels have changed since the Ice Age. When sea levels rose at the end of the Ice Age the water tables would also have risen, allowing river erosion to take place. As the sea levels fell, the water tables fell and the valleys were left dry.

The cross-sections of dry valleys make an interesting study. Figure F shows students measuring the right side of Kingstone Coombes to the south east of Ashbury – 2784. Figure G shows students measuring **terracettes** formed by soil creep on the side of Odstone Coombes near Ashbury (Figure B). Both photographs show the small detail of chalk landscapes.

Figure F: Kingstone Coombes dry valley

Figure G: Terracettes on Odstone Coombes

▼ Questions

1 Link up the sketch block diagram (Figure B) with the Ordnance Survey map extract (Figure A).
   a How high is the land at the top of the escarpment above Ashbury?
   b What is the grid reference where the B 4000 crosses the Ridgeway (Oxfordshire Circular Walks)?
   c Describe a walk along the Ridgeway from the grid reference to the top of Uffington Castle. ➡
   d Using the map and block diagram describe the differences between the Vale of the White Horse and the Lambourn Downs. ➡

2 Study Figure C. Draw a cross-section from Odstone Marsh (Farm) in grid square 2687 to the track at the edge of the trees at grid reference 297837. The length is 5 kilometres, the same as Figure C. Label the main features of the chalk scenery: physical features in one colour and human features in another.

3 Use Figure E to describe and explain the location of Woolstone. ➡

4 Study Figures F and G and describe the detail of the two dry valleys shown. (The trees are beech and the yellow field is oil seed rape.)

5 What are the students doing in each of the photographs, Figures F and G? What enquiries could they be following?

6 Summarise the different theories for the formation of dry valleys. Which one(s) do you support? ➡

Weather and climate: Scotland's depressions

Main activity

This exercise comprises analysis and interpretation of a weather satellite image, a cross-section and a satellite image of Scotland.

Key ideas

● There are distinct west/east climate contrasts.
● The west receives the Atlantic depressions and the east is a rain shadow area.
● Natural vegetation and farming are closely linked to the climate.

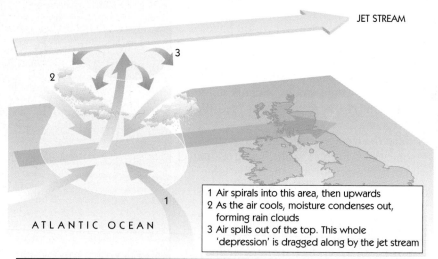

JET STREAM

1 Air spirals into this area, then upwards
2 As the air cools, moisture condenses out, forming rain clouds
3 Air spills out of the top. This whole 'depression' is dragged along by the jet stream

ATLANTIC OCEAN

Figure A: Depressions form over the Atlantic and are dragged along by the jet stream

Variability is the most striking feature of the Scottish climate. The weather can change daily, but average figures for weather over a long period of time give us climate data. The climate of the British Isles as a whole is **temperate** and there is a lack of extremes (the climate is **equable**). In Scotland two of Britain's climate types exist:

1 North West Britain which has cool summers, mild winters and heavy rain all year especially in winter
2 North East Britain which has cool summers, cold winters and is relatively dry all year.

Look at the weather satellite image (Figure B) which was taken in February.

M is the centre of the depression to the west of Ireland.
N is the occluded front.
O is the cold front.
P is the colder showery airstream behind the cold front.
Q is the warm front which in this case is small.
R is the warm sector between the cold and the warm fronts.

The depression is moving north east and will move across Scotland.

The British Isles are often referred to as the 'battleground of the air masses'. Scotland often bears the brunt of this battle. The depression has cold and wet polar maritime air being drawn down from the north west (**P**). To the south of the depression in the warm sector is tropical maritime air which is warmer. The depression is formed by this warmer air rising over the colder air and then cooling down. Figure B shows how the depression is dragged along by the upper atmosphere **jet stream** where continuous winds can exceed 160 kph/100 mph.

The effects of the depressions

Between September and January, depressions bring rainfall, cloud and high winds particularly to the west of Scotland. The rainfall graph for Tiree (Figure C) shows the seasonal rainfall variations. Figure D shows the much lower annual rainfall totals for Arbroath (for locations of Tiree and Arbroath see Figure E). Even in winter when the depressions are moving over Scotland there is little rainfall in Arbroath. In fact much of eastern lowland Scotland has low rainfall, similar to that in southern England counties such as Hampshire and Sussex. The reason for this is the **rain shadow** effect of the Scottish mountains. The winds descending the mountains towards the east are warming and therefore not rain-forming. The reason for the increased rainfall in summer in Arbroath is that there is some **convectional** rainfall in the warm summer temperatures.

Depressions come from the relatively warm Atlantic Ocean and therefore temperatures are rarely very low in west Scotland. The high relief in many parts of Scotland also affect the climate. Temperatures generally fall 0.6°C per 100 metres ascent, so it is considerably colder in the high mountain areas. As the air is rising and cooling over the mountains it is also more cloudy and wetter than in the lower areas. Winds are higher in the mountains and visibility worse. Snow cover is higher in the highest mountains. Braemar is near to the Cairngorm area at 339 metres above sea level. It has 59 days a year with snow lying at 9.00 a.m., Perth at 23 metres has 15 days and Tiree on the warmer west side at 9 metres has only 4 days.

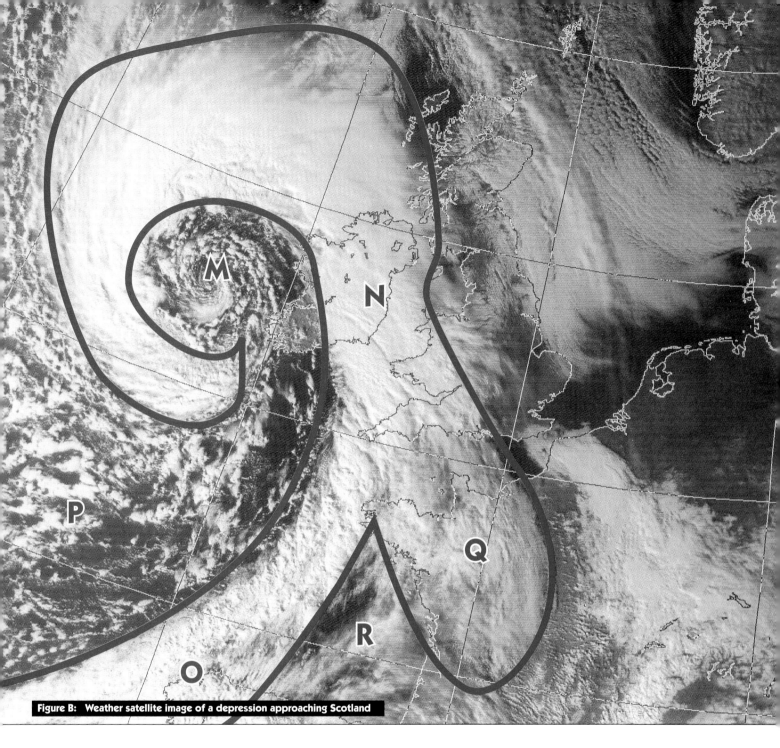

Figure B: Weather satellite image of a depression approaching Scotland

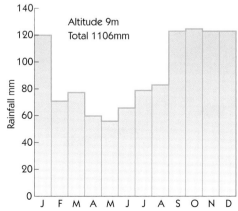

Altitude 9m
Total 1106mm

Rainfall mm

J F M A M J J A S O N D

Figure C: Rainfall graph for Tiree

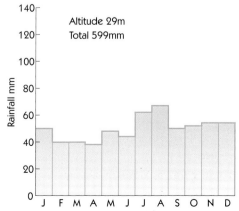

Altitude 29m
Total 599mm

Rainfall mm

J F M A M J J A S O N D

Figure D: Rainfall graph for Arbroath

CASE STUDY:
Weather and climate – Scotland west to east

The cross-section across Scotland (Figure F) shows the distinct contrasts between the west and the east. The west receives the moist depressions from the Atlantic Ocean. Here cloud amounts are greatest, rainfall heaviest, sunshine amounts lowest and winds strongest. It is the most exposed part of Britain; the outer Hebrides have strong winds (over 40 kph/25 mph) on one day in every three.

Line of section: Tiree to Arbroath

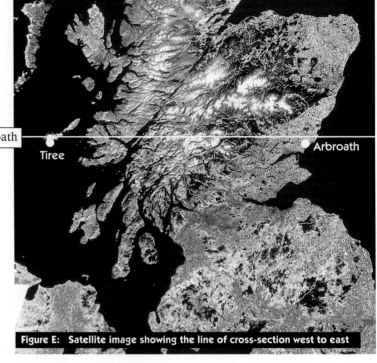

Tiree

Arbroath

Figure E: Satellite image showing the line of cross-section west to east

Location	Tiree	Fort William	Perth	Arbroath
Altitude (metres)	9	15	23	29
January average daily max. °C	7.2	6.3	5.7	5.7
January average daily min. °C	2.8	0.9	0.6	0.9
July average daily max. °C	15.8	17.2	19.1	18.1
July average daily min. °C	10.8	9.9	10.3	10.5
Annual average rainfall (mm)	1106	1981	739	599
Average sunshine (hours)	1400	1059	1309	1499

WEST COAST

Prevailing south west winds and Atlantic depressions

MOUNTAINS

Air has risen, cooled and condensed, giving rain

LOWLANDS

Much of the moisture in the air has been lost. This is a rain shadow area

EAST COAST

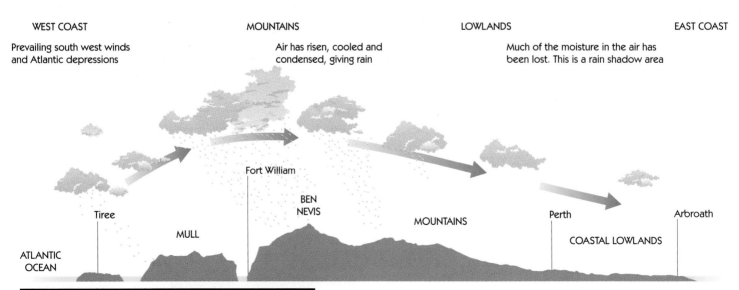

Fort William

BEN NEVIS

Tiree

MULL

MOUNTAINS

Perth

Arbroath

COASTAL LOWLANDS

ATLANTIC OCEAN

Figure F: West-east cross-section or transect across Scotland

Natural vegetation and farming

Scotland's natural vegetation was similar to that in much of central and western Europe. It consisted of mixed deciduous and coniferous forest. In parts of the Highlands there were forests of Scots pine. As with most places in Europe, it has been cut down and cleared. In the case of Scotland it was cut down from Bronze Age times, 2500 BC, for timber, fuel, building materials and farming. In 1997 a £1.4 million National Lottery grant was announced to re-establish natural trees over a 40-year programme. In the Glen Finglas Forest (south east of Perth and north of Aberfoyle) deciduous trees such as alder, rowan, birch, oak, ash and willow will be planted.

In the west of Scotland the wetter climate has created **acidic soils** some of which have turned to **peat**. Tree growth is restricted in the higher areas and the land is covered with heath and bog vegetation. In some of the highest areas Arctic alpine plants grow.

Patterns of farming

The map (Figure G) shows strong links between the growing season and east/west differences and highland/lowland areas. The growing season is the longest in the west. In brief, Scottish farming is a response to climate, soils and some cultural and social factors.

The wet west has favoured the growth of permanent grass and so dairy cattle are reared. Sheep have been important in Scotland since the land was 'cleared' of crofters in the nineteenth century in order to introduce sheep. Crops and beef rearing are important in the east where the climate is drier and there are easily worked, fertile and moderate to deep soils. Throughout Scotland there is little cultivated land over 300 metres where temperatures are lower, rainfall is higher and soils are shallower and more acidic.

Climate and natural vegetation change over the years and the global warming experts predict a 9% increase in rainfall by 2050 over the area shown on the cross-section. At the same time there could be more storms and gales over Scotland and temperatures could rise by 1.6°C (see map on page 6). Farming will respond to the climatic change and the east will become even more favourable to arable farming than it is at present.

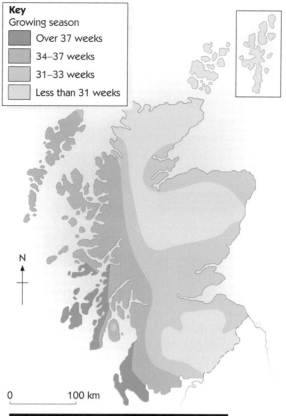

Key
Growing season

- Over 37 weeks
- 34–37 weeks
- 31–33 weeks
- Less than 31 weeks

N

0   100 km

Figure G: The average length of the growing season in Scotland

▼ Questions

1 What is a depression?
2 a What effects do depressions have on west Scotland?
  b Why do depressions have less effect on the east side of Scotland?
3 Attempt to draw a synoptic chart from the information given on the satellite image.
4 Describe and explain the differences between the pattern of rainfall for Tiree and Arbroath (Figures C and D).
5 Describe and explain the climate differences across the cross-section (Figure F). ➔
6 How is the growing season (Figure G) influenced by west/east differences and the highland/lowland divide in Scotland?

Review

Depressions have a greater influence on the west side of Scotland than on the east. There are distinct climate differences between west and east Scotland.

The threatened coast

Main activity

This is an introduction to coastal problems with data response questions and report writing on the example of building a beach at Seaford.

Key ideas

● Coasts and estuaries are often no longer natural physical features.
● Coasts are threatened by a range of developments, pollutants and leisure activities.
● Coasts can be protected and saved.

Figure A: The threats to the coast

There is still some coastline in the UK that is natural, but much of it has been developed or is threatened. Figures A and B show the threats to the coasts.

Figure B: Headlines reporting threats to the coast

Threats to the estuaries

There are about 160 river mouths or larger river estuaries in the UK and they are particularly vulnerable. They are sheltered water areas used for commercial shipping and pleasure boats. Access from the land is usually easy and they are often popular for leisure activities. Industry has located on the estuaries because of the available flat land and easy disposal of effluents and waste. Features of a typical estuary are shown in Figure D.

Many estuaries have been permanently damaged. If barrages are built across estuaries to generate electricity from the tides, then estuaries as we know them will be changed. The Cardiff Bay and Swansea Barrages, in South Wales, were built to create areas for boating and waterside developments. These have replaced the tidal estuaries with permanent freshwater lakes.

In 1994 an organisation called Coastwatch surveyed 1800 kilometres of coast. Figure C gives details of coastal pollution for three counties. Much of the litter had been thrown off ships and moved onto the coasts by currents, tides and longshore drift.

County	Glass	Packing straps	Dangerous containers	Paper drink containers	Sanitary items	Cans	Plastic bottles
Cornwall	3	4	1	3	5	13	19
Durham	2	1	<1	<1	10	10	7
Merseyside	4	3	1	13	95	22	25

Figure C: Average number of litter items recorded per kilometre of coast

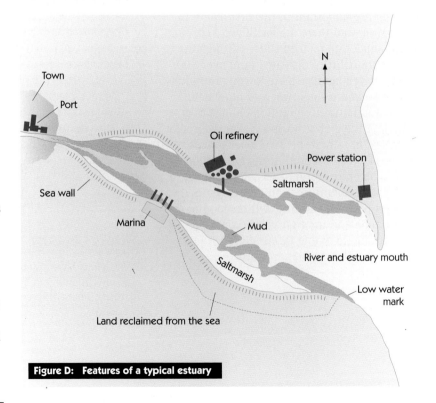

Figure D: Features of a typical estuary

Saving the coast

Careful management of the coasts and estuaries can result in **sustainable development**. This means there are close links between conservation *and* meeting the demand for leisure and other activities.

- English Nature have a 'Living Coast' campaign. A survey showed that 50% of the country's sand dunes are moving inland and are starved of sediment. This was once supplied from eroding cliffs that are now being protected by cliff engineering schemes.

- Money is still being spent protecting the coast at Hengistbury near Bournemouth, Dorset. In 1938 Bournemouth built a large groyne at Hengistbury Head to protect the cliffs by building up a beach. The groyne did collect beach material but it stopped the longshore drift moving it round to Christchurch Bay. Serious erosion took place beyond the protecting groyne. Bournemouth's action led to problems for the neighbouring local authority.

- The Commons Select Committee on the environment have stated that there is no overall planning for the coasts. The Local Authority planners only have power above the high tide mark. The authorities can not control what happens offshore.

- The Countryside Commission have identified 45 of the most outstanding stretches of coastline as Heritage Coasts. These now cover 35% of the coastline of England and Wales (Figure E). The aim is to protect the coast and to enhance people's enjoyment of them in 'sustainable' ways.

- The National Trust launched its Enterprise Neptune in 1965 with the aim of buying the coast to save it. In 1995 it owned 500 miles (800 kilometres) which it was actively protecting. At Easington, County Durham, a

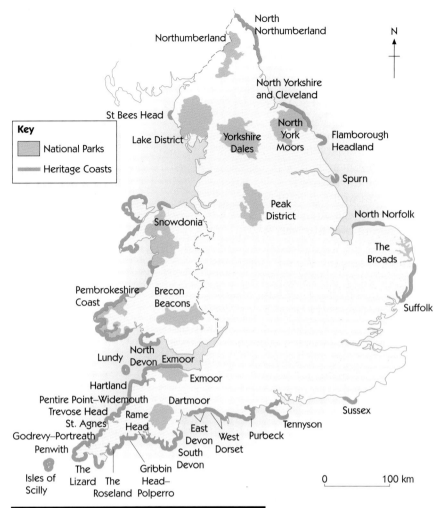

Figure E: The Heritage Coasts and the National Parks

coastline once blackened by a coal tip is now being restored.

- Some stretches of coastline are in National Parks and others are protected as SSSIs and AONBs (defined on page 25).

- The RSPB has coastal reserves. Its most visited reserve is Titchwell on the North Norfolk coast with over 100,000 visitors a year.

Do you know?

? The key ideas about coastal processes are *erosion*, *transportation* and *deposition*. Coastal engineers can affect these processes.

? Coasts are eroded by <u>c</u>orrasion, <u>a</u>ttrition, <u>s</u>olution, <u>h</u>ydraulic action (CASH). Erosion forms distinctive landforms.

? Eroded material is transported and deposited by *longshore drift*.

? Sand dunes may form, with marshy lagoons behind them where rivers deposit silt.

? Coastal erosion is reduced where there is beach material to absorb the wave energy. Coastline management has involved building sea walls and barriers, placing material at the foot of cliffs and building up beaches. Groynes allow beaches to retain material by trapping it as it moves along the beach. Sand dunes can be managed to stabilise them.

CASE STUDY: Saving Seaford

Figure F shows the exposed location of Seaford on the East Sussex coast. For years Seaford suffered storms with spray reaching heights of 20 metres that left several centimetres of shingle on the seafront road. A sea wall was built in 1881 but it was often damaged by waves of over five metres.

In 1987 the Dutch based dredging company, Zanen, started work on a beach replenishment scheme at Seaford. They built a new beach 2500 metres long and 115 metres wide. They took shingle from an offshore bank using a suction-hopper dredger *Barent Zanen* (Figure G). When the dredger was loaded it came to the submerged pontoon 800 metres offshore and pumped its shingle through the pipeline onto the beach.

The new beach material is kept in place by a large steel and concrete **groyne** built at the eastern end of Seaford beach (Figure H). Each year the material moves eastwards and builds up near the groyne – and is regularly taken back to the western end again!

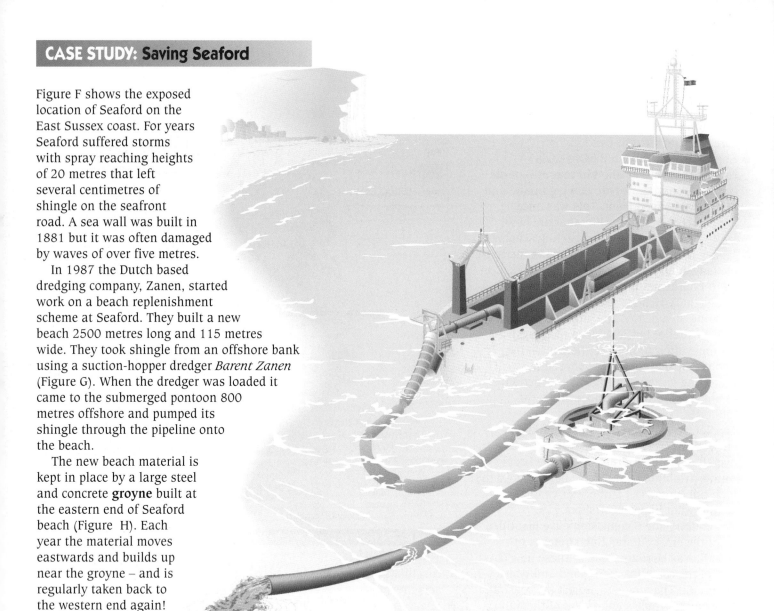

Figure G: Pumping gravel onshore to form a new beach

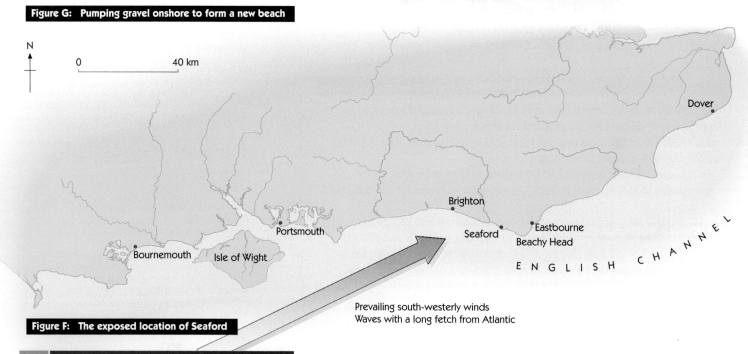

N

0   40 km

Dover

Brighton

Portsmouth

Seaford   Eastbourne
Beachy Head

Bournemouth   Isle of Wight

ENGLISH CHANNEL

Prevailing south-westerly winds
Waves with a long fetch from Atlantic

Figure F: The exposed location of Seaford

Figure H: Seaford beach being replenished with material

The new beach was a success. According to the *Seaford Gazette* (Figure I) the local environment has been improved, and the beach is a better tourist attraction and recreational resource for the local people.

SAVED!

£9m sea defences halt flood disaster

SEAFORD was saved from a flooding disaster by its new multi-million pound beach during the worst storms to hit the town in living memory.

Without the beach, Thursday night's violent seas would have crashed over the Esplanade and Marine Parade, causing total destruction to seafront houses and leaving the town flooded, say experts.

Figure I: From the Seaford Gazette, October 1987

▼ Questions

1. Study Figure A. Draw up a table to show how the coasts are threatened from agriculture, activities at sea and tourists.
2. Study Figure C. In what ways did the litter found on the coastlines of the three counties differ? What reasons can you give for the differences? (Start by locating these coastal areas in an atlas.)
3. Read the following scenario for the estuary shown in Figure D. 'Sea levels are slowly rising. Farmers want to reclaim more land from the sea in the area of the saltmarsh in the south where wintering birds feed. Planning permission is sought for a petrochemical plant to the east of the oil refinery.'
   Write a report on the possible future threats to this estuary. ➡
4. Make a list of the government bodies and other organisations who want to save the coast. For each give an example of their efforts.
5. What do you understand by **sustainable development** of the coast?
6. How have the coastal processes at Seaford been adjusted by human interference? Organise your answer using the following headings: Where is it? What was the problem? How have the natural processes been changed? What were the successes? ➡

Review

Coasts are rarely left to be natural physical features. They are threatened by a range of human and economic activities. They can be protected and managed by a variety of government and local initiatives.

Poole Harbour: Managing a coastal area

Figure A: Poole Harbour

Key ideas

● Poole Harbour is a fragile coastal environment under constant pressure from people's activities.
● It is an important wetland and coastal conservation area.
● Various organisations, government bodies and local councils try to manage the conflicting areas.

Main activity

This is a decision making exercise which includes background questions and suggestions for managing conflicting uses and development proposals.

Poole Harbour in Dorset, southern England, is Britain's largest natural harbour. At the water's edge of the harbour there is low lying wetland and marsh. The area is surrounded by heathland which has developed on sands and gravels. To the south are the chalk hills and cliffs of the Foreland with its sea stacks of Old Harry Rocks. These examples of sea erosion contrast with two features of sea deposition: the spits of Sandbanks and South Haven. The area is sheltered from the prevailing south west winds. The winters are mild, January 6°C, and the summers are warm, July 16°C. Sunshine totals are high for Britain with over 1700 hours a year (Birmingham 1300 hours, Kew 1500 hours).

The Harbour and its surrounding heathlands is one of the country's most important conservation areas. It is in a densely populated area with the Poole and Bournemouth built up areas spreading east from the eastern part of the

Harbour. The whole area is a 'honeypot' location for recreation and tourism.

The southern area overlays Britain's sixth largest oilfield, the largest onshore oilfield in western Europe (Figure B). The photograph (Figure A) the Ordnance Survey map (Figure C) and the map (Figure D) locate the present developments and the potentially conflicting land and water uses.

Figure B: A 'Nodding donkey' oil pump on the Wytch Farm oil field

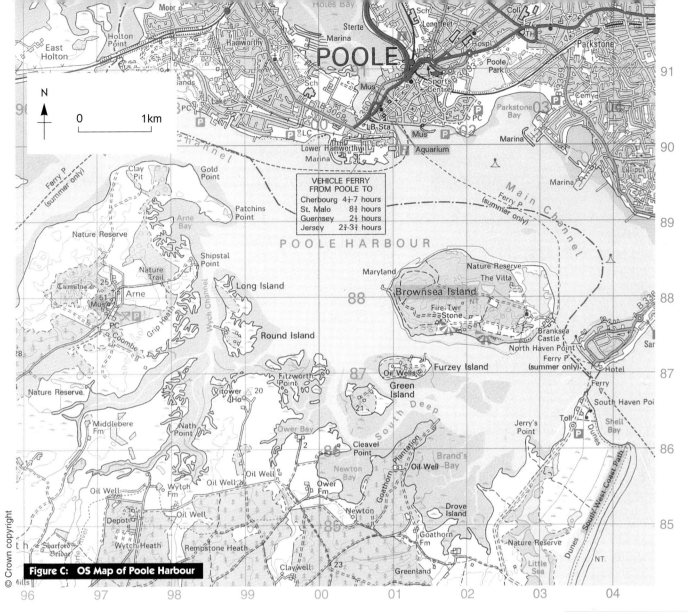

Figure C: OS Map of Poole Harbour

© Crown copyright

VEHICLE FERRY
FROM POOLE TO
Cherbourg 4¼-7 hours
St. Malo 8¾ hours
Guernsey 2¼ hours
Jersey 2¾-3¾ hours

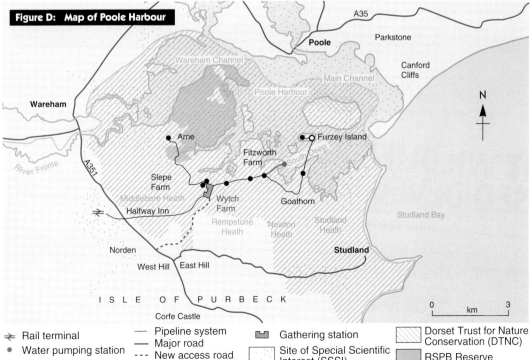

Figure D: Map of Poole Harbour

≽ Rail terminal
● Water pumping station
● Existing well sites
○ New well site

— Pipeline system
— Major road
--- New access road
— Area of outstanding Natural Beauty

▱ Gathering station
Site of Special Scientific Interest (SSSI)
National Nature Reserve

Dorset Trust for Nature Conservation (DTNC)
RSPB Reserve
Heritage Coast

▼ Questions

1 In which direction was the camera pointing in Figure A? Name the large island in the centre, the spit to the right, and the point from where the ferry is leaving.

2 Use the resources in this unit. Write a short report in which you state:
  a why Poole Harbour and the surrounding areas are such important conservation areas.
  b the ways in which the environment is protected.
  c the conflicting land and water uses.

Poole Harbour:
Conflicting uses and environmental pressures

Studland Heath and sand dunes

Problems
- Managed by English Nature under a lease from the National Trust
- Studland is a Heritage Coast
- All six species of British reptiles live here – 3 lizards and 3 snakes
- Rare heathland plants grow e.g. Dorset Heather
- 20,000 visitors can be on Studland Beach on a hot summer's day
- Most visitors arrive by car
- The road to the beach is also the road to the ferry which crosses to Sandbanks
- Up to 200 cars can be illegally parked on the roadside or on the fragile heath next to the road
- 400 yachts can 'overnight' in the bay producing unpleasant pollution
- A coastal path goes along the beach
- The beach is a resting place for winter migratory birds. Walkers can disturb them

Solutions
- Overflow car parks but no more are possible because of destroying more heathland
- Footpaths to follow the public's 'desire lines' – the routes they naturally follow
- Fences along roads to stop parking
- Ditches to stop 4x4 vehicles crossing the heath
- Prosecuting off-road motor cyclists
- Trying to set up a 'poop-scoop' scheme to stop dogs fouling the beaches
- Setting up a park-and-ride scheme
- Bring people into Studland on ferries from nearby towns

Poole Harbour and the surrounding wetlands

Problems
- About 18 different uses within the Harbour and 4000 boats can be using the harbour at a peak time
- Oil drilling and service boats between the islands
- A commercial port
- A cross-Channel ferry port with services to Cherbourg
- Boat services to the National Trust owned Brownsea Island
- A range of watersports
- Commercial shell-fishing with exports to France
- Private angling
- Bird watching. The area is internationally important for shelducks and black-tailed godwits. The RSPB reserve at Arne covers heathland and salt marsh.
- Wildfowl shooting
- Holiday-makers and day trippers
- More developments will increase threats to the natural environment (Figure D).

Solutions
- An aquatic management plan where different water uses are zoned and quiet areas are encouraged (Figures E and G)
- Encourage small boats and wind surfers to go out to sea rather than stay in the Harbour
- Build more safe marinas; these are safer than the old 'swinging' moorings (Figures E and H)
- Try to spread visitors throughout the year
- Regular management meetings of interested parties such as the local councils, Poole Harbour Commissioners and conservation groups
- Attract money from the EU

IMPORTANT WILDLIFE REFUGE THREATENED BY PROPOSED DEVELOPMENT

DIANA HENDERSON reports on the plight of important wintering waterfowl refuge threatened by proposed developments to Poole Harbour

NOWHERE is the conflict between nature and man brought into sharper focus than at popular and scenic places like Poole Harbour.

One of the world's largest natural harbours, its 10,000 acres of water attract thousands of watersports enthusiasts every year.

Around 30,000 people live along its northern shores and there is pressure for better roads, more watersports facilities and ever more development.

On the other side of the coin the vast expanses of water are home to more than 22,000 wintering waterfowl, it is of international importance for some species and has various levels of environmental protection.

But the dark cloud of development hangs over the harbour and the Poole Bridge replacement, Town Quay Boat Haven and the marina being built at Parkstone Yacht Club are setting conservationists' hearts fluttering.

Now Poole Harbour Commissioners (PHC) have instituted an Aquatic Managment Plan to try and iron out conflicts between a commercial port, recreational area and nature conservation.

From the Bournemouth Evening Echo, 9 February 1995

Figure E

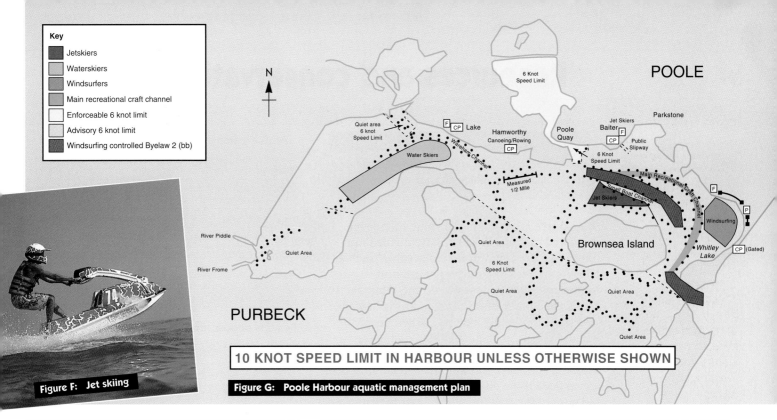

Key
- Jetskiers
- Waterskiers
- Windsurfers
- Main recreational craft channel
- Enforceable 6 knot limit
- Advisory 6 knot limit
- Windsurfing controlled Byelaw 2 (bb)

N

POOLE

6 Knot Speed Limit

Parkstone

Quiet area 6 knot Speed Limit

F CP Lake

Hamworthy Canoeing/Rowing CP

Poole Quay

Jet Skiers Baiter

CP F Public Slipway

6 Knot Speed Limit

Water Skiers

Wareham Channel

Measured 1/2 Mile

Main Recreational Craft Channel

Small Boat Channel

Jet Skiers

F

P

Windsurfing

River Piddle

River Frome

Quiet Area

Quiet Area

6 Knot Speed Limit

Quiet Area

Brownsea Island

Whitley Lake

CP (Gated)

Quiet Area

Quiet Area

PURBECK

10 KNOT SPEED LIMIT IN HARBOUR UNLESS OTHERWISE SHOWN

Figure G: Poole Harbour aquatic management plan

Figure F: Jet skiing

An artist's impression of the haven at Fisherman's Dock

An ambitious plan for an £8 million boat haven may be sunk if it is not supported by the council.

If the council refuses to back the scheme proposed by the Poole Harbour Commissioners, and donate the necessary land, the scheme would probably not be financially viable.

Opponents to the scheme, the Poole Harbour Action Group, say it would change the face of Poole Quay and hope the plan will go under.

Harbour commissioners Chief Executive Hamish Green says the scheme will be a massive boost for town traders.

Figure H: Adapted from the Bournemouth Evening Echo, July 1995

▼ Questions

1   You are a conservationist in a meeting with English Nature and the National Trust discussing the problems of Studland Beach. What are your points of view and suggestions on the following three agenda items?
   a   The problem of wintering birds on the beach at high tide. At this time the walkers use the very narrow beach just below the sand dunes as this is technically the long distance coastal path. There is no possibility of moving the path permanently but possibly a temporary path could be made through the sand dunes.
   b   The problem of young motorcyclists who ride around the heathland.
   c   Off-road parking which is harming the heathland immediately next to the road.

2   The Management and Planning Group for Poole Harbour is meeting to discuss the Aquatic Management Plan which was introduced in 1994. What is your opinion on the following applications? You must give your answer from the Management Group's point of view.
   a   The Jet Skiers Association have applied for a second zone. They want this to be near road access and near the town, off Lower Hamworthy.
   b   The Power Boat Racing Club want to start using the Harbour for flat water training. They have applied for their own zone.
   Suggest where in Poole Harbour the zones could be. When deciding on their location be careful not to overlap with shipping lanes and other users zones.

3   The Poole Harbour Commissioners put forward a plan for a new marina. Study Figures E and H. They state that it would be safer than the old moorings in the Harbour. It will bring in income. Once all the moorings have been let it would help control the numbers of boats using the harbour. PHAG, The Poole Harbour Action Group, is opposed to the plan. What are the arguments for *and* against the new marina?

Review

Despite the pressures on the Poole Harbour area careful management is preserving the natural environment and the economic and leisure activities. Firm decision making in the future will be essential. Sometimes the only right answer will be no more development.

Resources and conservation

Key ideas

● Using resources can have unintended effects on the environment.
● The UK's countryside is under pressure and attempts to conserve it are complex.
● Decision making processes can help to think through resource management issues.

Main activity

This is an exercise in learning to use a decision tree in order to help guide decision making.

A **resource** is something of value that people need and can use. Resources are divided into those that are **renewable** (replaceable) such as water and trees and those that are **non-renewable** such as fossil fuels and minerals. We use a wide range of resources but it is how we use them that really matters. When people misuse resources there are often damaging effects on the environment. In the case of Poole Harbour the coast and wetlands could have been devastated if the oil drilling had not taken account of the fragility of the environment. Tourist pressures could damage the sand dunes and the harbour itself unless careful planning and controls are followed. Yorkshire Water has to manage the natural water supplies in order to supply its customers. The Exmoor National Park authorities have to plan for visitors and provide amenities for them.

When there is a conflict of interest about how resources should be used and developed then there is an **issue**. There are many issues raised in this book; some are described along with the possible solutions, such as those in Poole Harbour and Exmoor. Some have been solved, such as the development of industrial wasteland in the Don Valley, Sheffield (page 84). In the case of the expansion of Birmingham Airport (page 82) the solutions will lead to other, more local issues which will need to be resolved.

Countryside under pressure

● Leisure activities are expanding in rural areas as people become more affluent and mobile. Places where large crowds of people gather, such as natural or cultural features, are known as **honeypots**.
● The ownership of second homes has brought changes and problems to people living in the rural areas. House prices have risen in second home areas and local people have found it difficult to buy their own homes.
● Towns have spread into the countryside although there has been a **Green Belt Policy** since the 1940s.

Figure A gives some results from a recent poll by the Countryside Commission. More than half of

People's thoughts about the countryside

I believe the countryside is an important part of our heritage	**91%**
Society has a moral duty to protect the countryside for future generations	**91%**
The English countryside should be protected at all costs	**89%**
People would really appreciate more natural open space in and around towns and cities	**87%**
The countryside is an important part of my life	**85%**
Population growth in this country means that towns and cities will have to expand into the countryside	**78%**

Benefits people see in visiting the countryside

Relaxation/well-being	**45%**
Fresh air	**24%**
Peace and quiet	**22%**
Fitness	**14%**

Where people would like to live

Currently live	Inner city	Suburb	Town	Countryside
Countryside	0%	7%	4%	89%
Town	1%	13%	46%	39%
Suburb	2%	47%	8%	43%
Inner city	21%	18%	10%	51%

Figure A: Views on the countryside, from a poll conducted by the Countryside Commission

the English population would like to live in the countryside. There is a conflict of interest here. Who is the countryside for? How can this issue be solved? The Council for the Preservation of Rural England have produced maps to show the shrinking of England's tranquil areas – those areas beyond the immediate influence of towns, roads, airports, overhead pylons and mining (Figure B). There has been a 14% decline in tranquil areas over three decades with the south east losing out most with a 20% decline. How can the loss of tranquility be reduced? Some of the conservation measures which exist to protect the countryside and wildlife are summarised in Figure D.

Figure C: The village of Upper Snodsbury, a lowland settlement

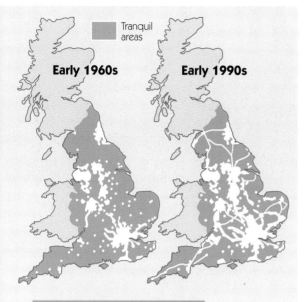

Tranquil areas

Early 1960s **Early 1990s**

Tranquil areas are measured as:

- 4 km from a power station
- 3 km from major motorways, large towns and major industrial areas
- 2 km from major trunk roads and the edge of smaller towns
- 1 km from busy roads and main line railway lines
- beyond military and civilian airfield noise
- beyond sight of open cast mining

Figure B: The loss of England's tranquil areas

Using a decision tree

There are many occasions when you are faced with questions such as 'What can be done to resolve the issue?', 'What is the solution to the problem?' Using a decision tree can help you think through the options. You can then work out the likely 'costs' and 'benefits' of each option. Figure E shows a possible decision tree on the problem of loss of tranquillity if a new by-pass is built in a rural area. Perhaps you can add to it.

Who deals with conservation?

The Countryside Commission The government's adviser on the conservation of the English countryside and its enjoyment by the people. For Wales a similar body is the Countryside Council for Wales.

English Nature The advising body for nature conservation and for promoting wildlife and natural features.

The Environment Agency It looks after rivers and coasts including amenity and recreation and has duties for conservation.

The National Trust A charitable organisation; the country's largest private landowner.

The Royal Society for the Protection of Birds (RSPB) A charitable organisation owning reserves and protecting bird habitats.

Designated areas

National Parks Ten parks set up in 1949 covering 10% of land and 10% of coasts. The Norfolk Broads designated in 1989. No National Parks in Scotland but Natural Heritage Areas set up in 1991.

Areas of Outstanding Natural Beauty Over 40 in England and Wales designated to protect important landscapes.

Heritage Coasts 45 designated coasts covering 35% of the coastline.

Sites of Special Scientific Interest (SSSIs) Strictly controlled for the protection of rare species of fauna or flora.

National Nature Reserves For very special conservation.

National Forest Parks Parks in forested areas of Britain.

Country Parks Small parks in and around urban areas for the enjoyment of local people.

Figure D: Who deals with conservation?

▼ Questions

1. Give an example of:
   a   renewable resource
   b   a non-renewable resource.
2. What is an environmental issue?
3. Give an example of the misuse of a resource which has developed into an environmental issue.
4. Why is the countryside under pressure?
5. Write a summary of English people's view of the countryside.
6. Design a decision tree on the problem of a 'honeypot' location on the coast. Start with the problem of 'Overcrowding on a summer's day at the sand dunes' then proceed with the options of 'Reducing the attractiveness of the honeypot' or 'Increasing the capacity of the honeypot'.

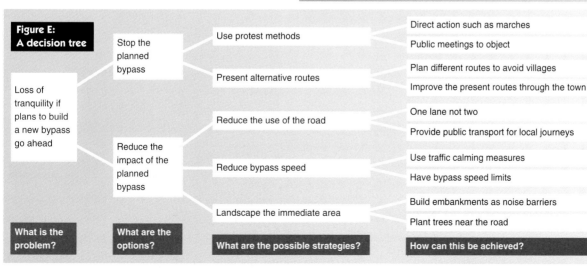

Figure E: A decision tree

What is the problem?	What are the options?	What are the possible strategies?	How can this be achieved?
Loss of tranquility if plans to build a new bypass go ahead	Stop the planned bypass	Use protest methods	Direct action such as marches / Public meetings to object
		Present alternative routes	Plan different routes to avoid villages / Improve the present routes through the town
	Reduce the impact of the planned bypass	Reduce the use of the road	One lane not two / Provide public transport for local journeys
		Reduce bypass speed	Use traffic calming measures / Have bypass speed limits
		Landscape the immediate area	Build embankments as noise barriers / Plant trees near the road

Review

The countryside is a resource under pressure. Finding solutions to environmental issues can be helped by using a decision tree.

Rivers and water supply

If you look in an atlas you will find maps of the distribution of rainfall in the British Isles and the distribution of population. There is a mismatch; it rains most in the higher areas of the north and west but most of the population live in the lower areas of the east and south. Some of the higher rainfall areas do supply water to population centres. Reservoirs in mid-Wales supply Birmingham and Liverpool; the Lake District sends water to Manchester from lakes such as Thirlmere and Hawes Water. The south and east of England have the most **underground aquifers**. London's water comes from the underground chalk **syncline** known as an **artesian basin**.

In 1974 a National Water Plan suggested large scale water transfer using aqueducts and rivers to convey water. It proposed a barrage across the River Dee in North Wales to store estuary water. The plan was never carried out. Today there are some regional transfers of water such as the Kielder Scheme.

The drainage basin

The drainage basin needs to be understood as a **system**. It has inputs and outputs, and processes going such as water treatment, wildlife conservation and flood control schemes. It is the basic unit of management for a water company and for the Environment Agency. This is the government organisation which is responsible for protecting and improving the water environment in England and Wales. Figure A summarises all the features of a

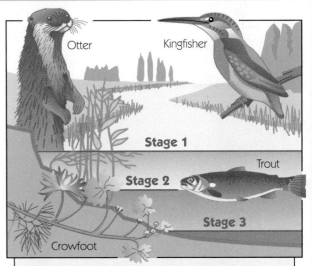

Stage 1
As water levels fall, plants at the side wither and cover for otters, voles and birds disappears. Oxygen concentration falls and water temperature rises. Freshwater plants (e.g. crowfoot) and insects (e.g. water boatmen, mayflies) die. Fish (e.g. trout) move to find better conditions.

Stage 2
As water levels fall further, pollution becomes more concentrated, affecting bottom-living fish (e.g. roach), snails and crayfish. Concentration of fertilisers and insecticides causes algal blooms which poison river life. Any effluents cannot be diluted.

Stage 3
The river dies.

Figure A: A river can die if too much water is taken out

drainage basin relating to the supply of water and the management of its water environment.

▼ Questions

1 Study Figure B.
   a In three columns write down the inputs, processes and outputs for the drainage basin system.
   b Identify some problems with the water quality.
   c How could the water quality be improved?
   d State some of the improvements being made to prevent flooding.
   e In what ways is recreation being planned on the lower river?
   f How could the tidal areas be conserved and protected?
2 Study Figure A. State briefly why there are limits on the amount of water a water company can extract from a river.

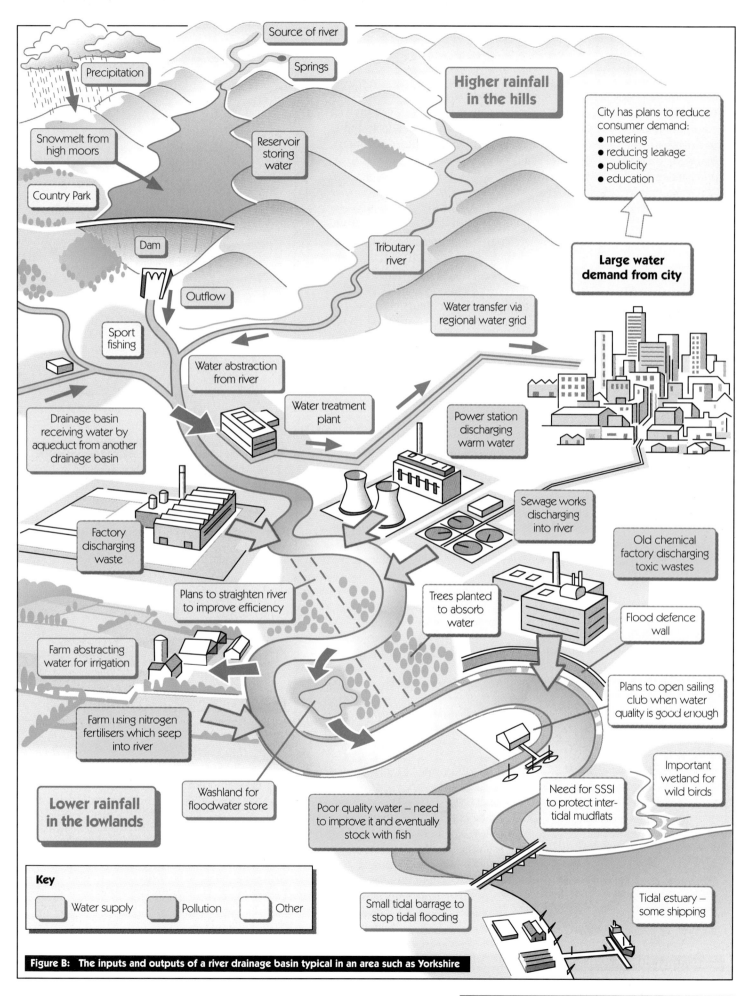

Figure B: The inputs and outputs of a river drainage basin typical in an area such as Yorkshire

Precipitation

Source of river

Springs

Higher rainfall in the hills

City has plans to reduce consumer demand:
● metering
● reducing leakage
● publicity
● education

Snowmelt from high moors

Reservoir storing water

Country Park

Tributary river

Dam

Large water demand from city

Outflow

Water transfer via regional water grid

Sport fishing

Water abstraction from river

Drainage basin receiving water by aqueduct from another drainage basin

Water treatment plant

Power station discharging warm water

Factory discharging waste

Sewage works discharging into river

Old chemical factory discharging toxic wastes

Plans to straighten river to improve efficiency

Trees planted to absorb water

Flood defence wall

Farm abstracting water for irrigation

Plans to open sailing club when water quality is good enough

Farm using nitrogen fertilisers which seep into river

Important wetland for wild birds

Lower rainfall in the lowlands

Washland for floodwater store

Poor quality water – need to improve it and eventually stock with fish

Need for SSSI to protect inter-tidal mudflats

Key

Water supply   Pollution   Other

Small tidal barrage to stop tidal flooding

Tidal estuary – some shipping

CASE STUDY: Yorkshire Water

Key ideas

● People in Yorkshire use water that comes from three sources.
● The water company has to balance supply and demand. Drought has been a major problem.
● Water quality is affected by a large population and heavy industries. Solutions need to be found for flooding.

Main activity

This is an exercise about water management with questions on the variables of water supply and demand, and the costs and benefits of pollution control and flood management.

Yorkshire Water plc serves a region of 4.5 million people (Figure A). The region includes some densely populated cities where the drain and sewer system, the **water infrastructure**, is now old. There is extensive heavy industry in the south and west including textiles and heavy chemicals. Figure B shows the three main sources of water in Yorkshire. About 3% is 'imported' from the neighbouring Severn Trent region. In future, water may also be brought in from the north.

Figure C shows both the location of the water supply and the demand for it. Water is supplied to customers from the three main sources of water through a grid system which was started in the 1960s. There are over 100 reservoirs which are mainly in the wetter and more hilly areas of the west. Their main function is to store water but nearly all have public access and many are used for fishing, sailing and general leisure. There are reservoirs in Yorkshire's three National Parks.

Figure A: The ten water and sewerage companies

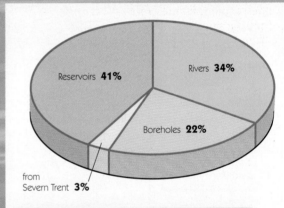

Figure B: The main sources of water in Yorkshire

Water for Leeds

There are over 670,000 people in the Leeds built-up area. They receive water from the Washburn valley to the north (Figure C). If there were a problem with this direct supply then Leeds can receive water from other sources via the water transmission grid. The map and photograph (Figure D) give details about the Washburn valley. The reservoirs were built over 100 years ago and are in the Nidderdale Moors which is now a proposed Area of Outstanding Natural Beauty (AONB).

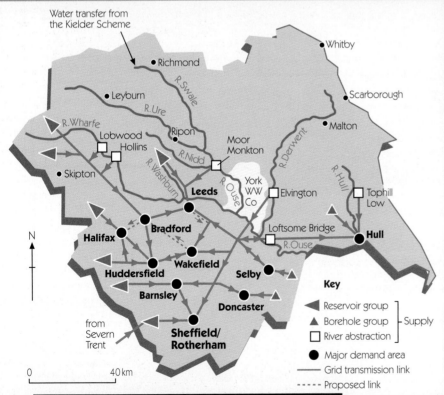

Figure C: The location of water supply and demand in Yorkshire

Drought and the management of supply and demand

Yorkshire does not usually suffer **drought** but 1995 was the driest time for over 100 years. Thruscross Reservoir was only 29% full (Figure E). While the supply of water was much lower than usual, the demand was higher.

The following measures were taken to cope with the problem.

- The use of hosepipes was banned
- Bottled water was produced
- Water was transported around Yorkshire by tankers
- Fountains were switched off
- People were encouraged to use water carefully
- Plans were made to build a pipeline to bring water from Kielder Reservoir in north east England (Figure F)
- Applications were made to take more water out of rivers. If too much water is taken from rivers serious damage can be done to them (Figure B, page 26).

About one-third of all the water that flows through very old water mains is lost by leakage. Yorkshire Water says that it would be uneconomic to reduce that figure much below one-quarter. The consumers find this difficult to understand; it is one of several criticisms made of the water company.

Figure E: West End village

Figure F: Plans for the pipeline from Kielder Reservoir (from The Times, 15 November, 1995)

Government plans to pipe water to drought-hit area

By Paul Wilkinson

A PIPELINE linking Yorkshire with the abundant water supplies of northeast England is to be built to stave off future shortages affecting millions of consumers. But the link, announced yesterday by David Curry, an Environment Minister, at the end of a tour of the affected parts of West Yorkshire, will not stave off possible rota cuts.

The pipe would be used to top up Yorkshire reservoirs during the winter. The link will run ten kilometres from the River Tees in the Northumbrian Water Region to the River Swale in North Yorkshire. Mr Curry said that the Government would provide every facility to ensure that the pipeline would be operating within the shortest possible time.

It will enable Yorkshire Water, which so far this year has received less than half its average rainfall, to tap into the vast reserves of Kielder Water, Europe's largest manmade lake high in the Cheviots. Supplies from Kielder would be transferred via Northumbria's system into the Tees. Once it is pumped across to the Swale it can be fed into Yorkshire's water grid.

However, Yorkshire Water later said that the pipeline was only one of a number of "medium-term options" it was examining.

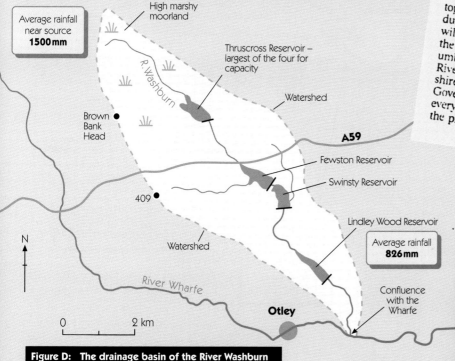

Figure D: The drainage basin of the River Washburn showing the four storage reservoirs

Average rainfall near source **1500 mm**

High marshy moorland

R. Washburn

Thruscross Reservoir – largest of the four for capacity

Watershed

Brown Bank Head

A59

409

Fewston Reservoir

Swinsty Reservoir

Lindley Wood Reservoir

Average rainfall **826 mm**

Watershed

N

River Wharfe

Otley

Confluence with the Wharfe

0   2 km

Thruscross Reservoir below 30% capacity in 1995. The former West End village was exposed

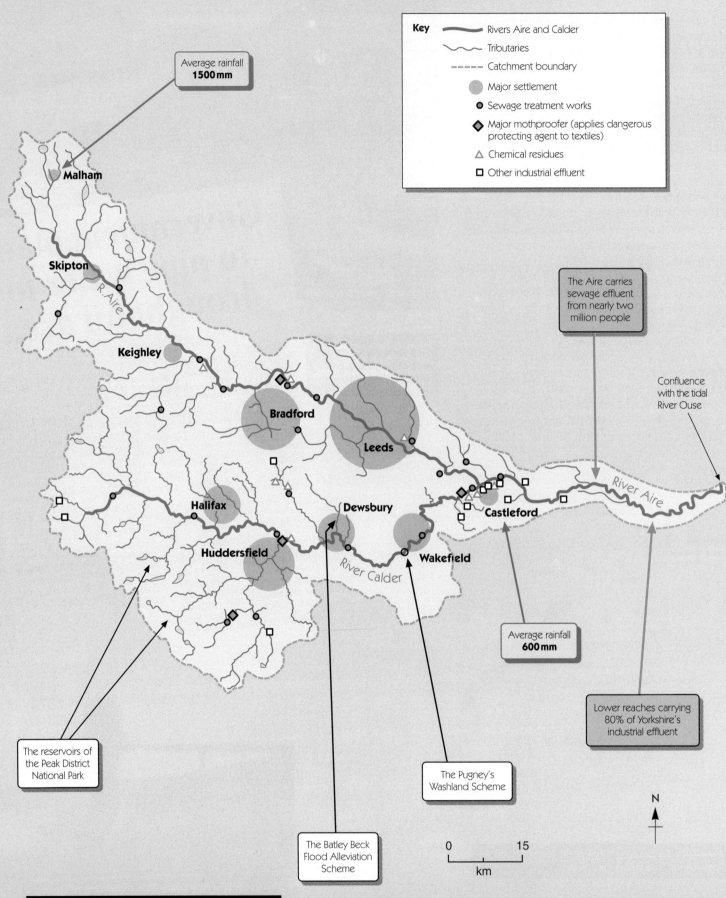

Key
~~~ Rivers Aire and Calder
~~~ Tributaries
--- Catchment boundary
● Major settlement
◉ Sewage treatment works
◆ Major mothproofer (applies dangerous protecting agent to textiles)
△ Chemical residues
□ Other industrial effluent

Average rainfall **1500 mm**

Malham

Skipton

R. Aire

Keighley

Bradford

Leeds

The Aire carries sewage effluent from nearly two million people

Confluence with the tidal River Ouse

River Aire

Halifax

Dewsbury

Castleford

Huddersfield

River Calder

Wakefield

Average rainfall **600 mm**

Lower reaches carrying 80% of Yorkshire's industrial effluent

The reservoirs of the Peak District National Park

The Pugney's Washland Scheme

The Batley Beck Flood Alleviation Scheme

0   15
km

N

Figure G: The Rivers Aire and Calder drainage basin

Unlike the rivers to the north, no water is taken out of the Aire and Calder (Figure G) although there are many reservoirs on the small tributaries. Below Leeds and Huddersfield, most of the river water in these rivers is of poor to bad quality, and there are few fish. Figure H summarises the problems.

What are the sources of the industrial pollution?

The legacy of industry from the Industrial Revolution such as chemical manufacturing plants and textile works (originally wool). The high density of urban population.

What is the environmental impact of this pollution?

Unacceptable colour of the water which can result from textile dyes. Residues from detergents used to wash textiles. Mothproofing insecticides used to protect textiles. Foul smells. Lack of oxygen concentrations and no river life.

How can pollution be controlled?

The Environment Agency must give permission for effluents to be discharged in a river. The Aire and Calder Minimisation Project involves industry and local authorities. Its aim is to reduce the amount of water used by industry and the amount of effluent it produces. Companies participating have saved money. Building modern sewage treatment works to replace old and inefficient ones which often combined sewers and water run-off. Providing refuse sites to deter people from dumping their rubbish in the river channels.

What are the costs and benefits of controlling pollution?

It is expensive for companies. They may have to raise the prices of their goods. If companies become unprofitable they will not employ so many people. Pollution kills river life. There are no water sports on polluted rivers. Rivers can become a health hazard. The benefits include saving money for companies, and improving leisure opportunities on the rivers, such as fishing if there are fish.

Figure H: The problems and control of river pollution

▼ Questions

1 a What are the three sources of water which supply the people of Yorkshire?

  b Using Figure C, describe how the water can be moved from the supply areas to the demand areas.

2 a Using Figure C, describe in detail how the city of Leeds is supplied with water.

  b If the supply of water to Leeds shown in Figure C dried up, in what other ways could Leeds receive water?

3 Write an article for a Yorkshire Water magazine detailing how the company dealt with the 1995 drought.

4 Why is the Aire and Calder drainage basin (Figure G) so polluted in its lower reaches?

5 The Board of Directors of a large chemical works on the River Aire have been approached by the Environment Agency about their waste water. They have to follow new discharge procedures. The Board is discussing the costs and benefits of the proposed new waste water discharge process. Discuss the proposals in a small group or as a class. Write down the arguments for and against the new process.

Figure I: Textile mills are one of many sources of pollution in Yorkshire

Yorkshire Water: managing and controlling floods in the Aire and Calder drainage basin

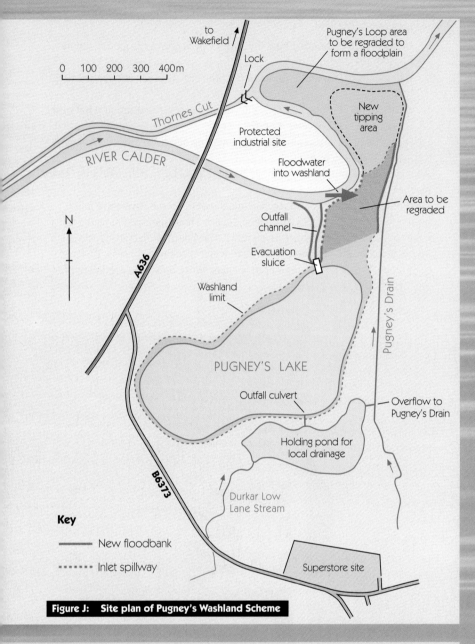

Figure J: Site plan of Pugney's Washland Scheme

Key

—— New floodbank

······ Inlet spillway

to Wakefield

0 100 200 300 400m

Thornes Cut

RIVER CALDER

A636

B6373

Lock

Pugney's Loop area to be regraded to form a floodplain

Protected industrial site

New tipping area

Floodwater into washland

Area to be regraded

Outfall channel

Evacuation sluice

Washland limit

PUGNEY'S LAKE

Outfall culvert

Pugney's Drain

Overflow to Pugney's Drain

Holding pond for local drainage

Durkar Low Lane Stream

Superstore site

1 The Pugney's Washland Scheme

The construction of **washlands** along the rivers Aire and Calder has reduced flooding. These low lying areas alongside rivers are reserved to take floodwater. The washland is poor quality grassland and lake; it is better for this to be flooded than higher quality farmland or urban areas. Figure J shows the river Calder south of Wakefield (indicated on Figure G). When floodwater comes down the Calder it is taken into Pugney's washland through the inlet spillway. When it is possible to release it, the water is let out of the outlet evacuation sluice. The benefits of the scheme outweigh the investment costs and the costs of having valuable land and property damaged because of flooding. The map also shows a holding pond and the outlet overflow to Pugney's Drain and the washland.

2 The Batley Beck Flood Alleviation Scheme

In 1996 a flood alleviation scheme was opened along the Batley Beck, a tributary of the river Calder at Dewsbury (indicated on Figure G). Half of its length is in culverts (artificial channels). Floods along its 7-kilometre length through the heavily urbanised area should no longer be a problem.

The problems were:
● Floods (Figure L)

The causes were:
● The inadequate size of the culverts
● The roughness of the river bed and banks
● Blockages in the culverts

The solutions (at a cost of £20 million) were:
● Lowering the river bed
● Paving the lowered river bed
● Underpinning existing walls
● Removing obstructions
● Replacing small and damaged culverts
● Constructing flood walls and barriers

Existing willow trees to be retained

New floodwall

New floodwall

Road

New concrete foundation to watercourse

Existing watercourse

Material excavated to increase the size of the channel

Figure K: A typical cross-section of a new part of the Batley Beck

Figure L: Floods in the urban area near Batley Beck before the Flood Alleviation Scheme

Figure M: New debris screens in the Batley Beck

Review

Many schemes exist in Yorkshire to balance an unreliable supply of water and a growing demand. Water quality is being improved but this requires investment and cooperation. Flood management can also be seen in terms of costs and benefits.

▼ Questions

6 Describe the location of the Pugney's Washland Scheme (Figures G and J) and explain how it works.

7 a Describe the location of the Batley Beck Flood Alleviation Scheme (Figure G).

   a What were the causes of local flooding?

   c How has flooding been controlled?

   d Justify spending £20 million to stop local flooding in Batley and Dewsbury.

CASE STUDY: Teesside and Kielder Water

Main activity

This exercise on resources for industry involves an analysis of an OS map and a satellite image, responding to a reservoir map, and creating an advertisement for the Development Corporation.

Key ideas

● Some of the resources used by the old heavy industries of Teesside are no longer needed.
● Resources must now be used with minimum environmental impact. Water is a key resource for modern industry.
● The multi-purpose Kielder Water scheme has provided a reliable water supply.

This study is about a heavy industrial area located on a river estuary. As the more traditional industries have declined newer ones have been established. Today there is concern for the natural environment of the estuary, and positive steps are being taken to conserve it. Water from the Kielder Reservoir in Northumberland is helping the region to modernise.

The resources for industry

From the 1850s the iron and steel industry developed on Teesside; over 800 iron furnaces opened between 1860 and 1880. The Cleveland Hills to the south supplied iron ore and the Durham coalfield provided coking coal.

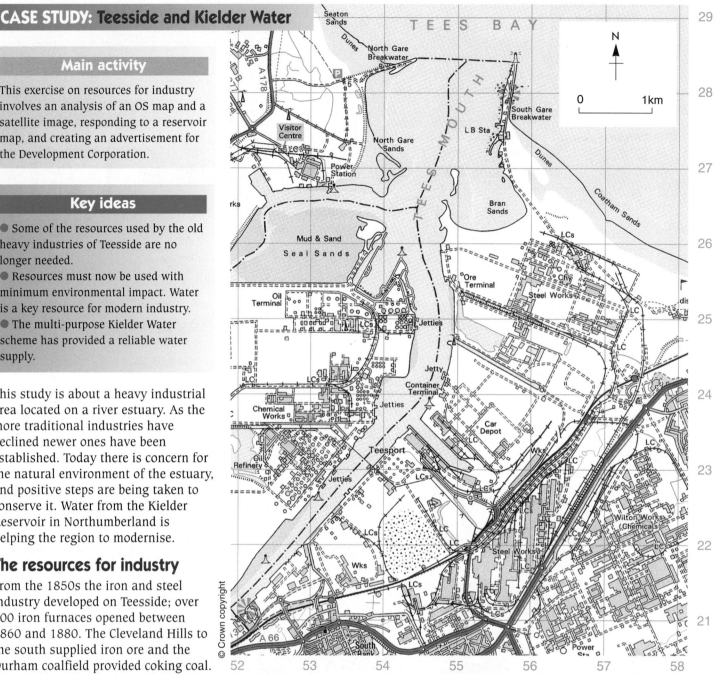

© Crown copyright

Figure B: The extent of the capital intensive industry around the mouth of the Tees

Figure A: Tees Estuary — oil refinery, Seal Sands

Limestone came from Durham and North Yorkshire. Today there is only one iron and steel works; iron ore is imported into a deep water iron ore terminal at grid reference 549255 on the map (Figure B). Coal is also imported because the Durham coalfield has now shut down. Iron is made at Redcar and the molten iron is taken to the steel plant at Lackenby where it is converted into steel slabs and castings. The limestone is the only raw material supplied locally. The original reasons for the siting of the iron and steel industry no longer apply but some sites remain as an example of **industrial inertia**.

The history of chemicals on Teesside goes back to the First World War when fertilisers were made there. Sulphur was obtained from anhydrite which was mined under Billingham. Coal was also used in the processes. Today the chemical factory at Billingham imports its raw materials – another example of industrial inertia.

The chemical industry still relies on the area's massive salt deposits some 300 metres below the surface. Water is pumped down boreholes, and dissolves the salt to make brine. This is pumped to the chemical works. Potash is mined at Boulby on the coast to the south east.

Oil and gas are the newer resources on which the heavy industries rely. There is an oil pipeline from the Ekofisk oil field in the North Sea. There are oil refineries and petrochemicals on the reclaimed mudflats. At Wilton there is a new gas-fired power station. Water from the Tees has always been used in both the iron and steel and chemical industries. Polluted water has been discharged into the river estuary. The estuary itself is a valuable resource; it has deep tidal water and mudflats which have been extensively reclaimed.

Resources and the environment

There was little concern for the environment during the Industrial Revolution when coal-powered iron making started and the area became the centre for the first steam railway (the Stockton to Darlington). Today the Tees is one of the most heavily used industrialised estuaries in the country with 90% of its former inter-tidal mudflat and saltmarsh reclaimed from the sea. The Ordnance Survey map (Figure B) shows the extent of the heavy industry, which is very **capital intensive**. The estuary has a National Nature Reserve, five SSSIs and a Special Protection Area for Birds and a Wetland of International Importance. Some 20,000 waterfowl visit the estuary each year. Since 1995 there has been a Teesside Estuary Management Plan which was drawn up by conservation organisations and industrial users.

Figure C shows an example of a recent investment by ICI to protect the environment. When ICI and its partners Enron and Amoco sink new brine wells they consult with English Nature. Part of Brinefield 6 is on the Teesmouth National Nature Reserve. Conservation measures include:
- re-creating **inter-tidal mudflats** and **lagoons**
- building floating islands to encourage terns to nest (Figure D)
- laying roads in gravel rather than asphalt so the ringed plover can nest more productively than it could on the beaches. (On the beach only 3% of eggs hatched but on gravel roads the success rate is 12%.)

Figure C: The ICI Sulphuric Acid Recovery Project at Billingham. This will save the Tees from 200,000 tonnes of acidic effluent each year

Figure D: Tern nesting raft on the 50-acre reservation at 553248 on the Ordnance Survey map (Figure B)

New industrial development

Teesside has been a Development Area since the 1930s when regional policy was set up. Since then successive governments have tried to assist the regions with grants and other incentives. Teesside Urban Development Corporation, set up in 1987, has the largest continuous area of de-industrialised land in Europe. Water has been an important resource in attracting new industry. While some areas of the country have been short of water in recent dry years, Teesside has reliable supplies from the Kielder Reservoir in Northumberland. Figure E on page 36 is an advertisement for Northumbrian Water.

Kielder Water

Samsung opened a new factory on Teesside in 1995. It makes microwave ovens, computer monitors and colour televisions. Suppliers of components for Samsung have also been attracted to the area.

Why Samsung chose the Wynyard site

- British Government Regional Aid support
- Local Authority assistance
- Teesside Development Corporation support
- Favourable experience at a smaller Billingham site
- Highly trained workforce
- Higher unemployment rates than nationally
- English language spoken (top international language)
- Efficient on-site infrastructure
- Reliable water supplies
- Lower wage rates than in southern England
- Closeness to European markets
- Port facilities on the Tees
- Modern road communications
- Nearby international airport

Water from Kielder

The Kielder Reservoir in Northumberland is Britain's largest artificial lake and was opened in 1982. There was a large grant from the European Regional Development Fund. Many people said the scheme was a waste of money as it was constructed to supply water to the heavy industries of Tyneside and Teesside. These industries were fast closing down and people could not see why the water was needed. The dam is over a kilometre long and the lake is 52 metres at its deepest point and holds 200,000 litres. Kielder supplies water to north east England and recently to Yorkshire (Figure F). The Reservoir area also has many other functions (Figure G).

Every plant needs water to grow

High on the shopping list of new expanding industries in the North East is availability of abundant supplies of high quality water. Over the years, Northumbrian Water built an excellent record for working with industry and a reputation for quality and reliability.

Right now a whole range of industries from chemical to automotive, electronics to pharmaceuticals, have successfully established themselves here - proving the value of water in a region's development.

NORTHUMBRIAN WATER
Owners of Kielder Water

Figure E: An advertisement for Northumbrian Water

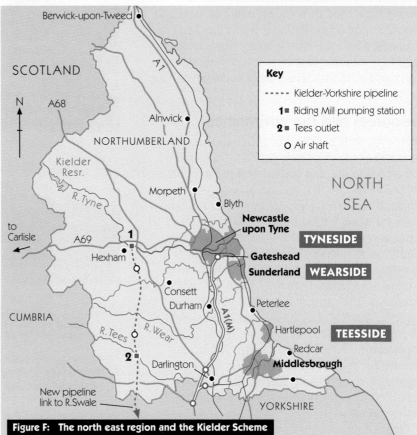

Key
- - - - - Kielder-Yorkshire pipeline
1 ■ Riding Mill pumping station
2 ■ Tees outlet
O Air shaft

Figure F: The north east region and the Kielder Scheme

Building the reservoir

Considerable environmental disruption was caused by the building of the reservoir.
- A remote valley was lost
- 70 dwellings were drowned
- 8 historical sites were drowned
- Salmon breeding grounds were lost
- Half a million trees were felled
- Construction work was disruptive.

On the other hand there was compensation.
- A multi-purpose lake was created
- A new road was built
- New homes in a nearby village were built
- Historical sites were studied before drowning
- A salmon hatchery was set up
- Trees were planted in greater variety
- Lake birds were attracted
- Thousands of people can enjoy the lake area.

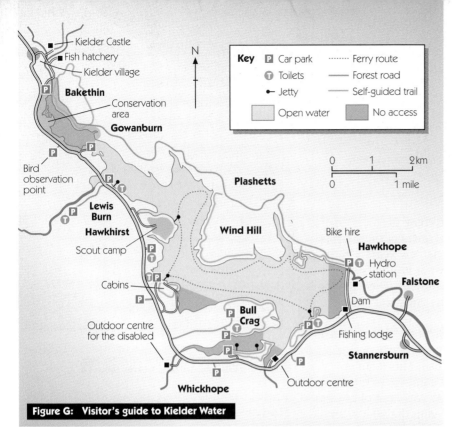

Key
- **P** Car park
- **T** Toilets
- • Jetty
- Open water
- ······· Ferry route
- Forest road
- Self-guided trail
- No access

N

Kielder Castle
Fish hatchery
Kielder village
Bakethin
Conservation area
Gowanburn
Bird observation point
Lewis Burn
Hawkhirst
Scout camp
Cabins
Outdoor centre for the disabled
Whickhope
Plashetts
Wind Hill
Bull Crag
Bike hire
Hawkhope
Hydro station
Falstone
Dam
Fishing lodge
Stannersburn
Outdoor centre

0   1   2km
0   1 mile

Figure G: Visitor's guide to Kielder Water

Figure H: Satellite false colour image of north east England

Questions

1 List the local resources used in Teesside's industry in a table similar to the one below.

Resource	Its use	Currently used
Iron ore	Making iron	No, now imported
Coking coal		

2 Study the Ordnance Survey map (Figure B).
Either:
a List the industries named and describe the landscape of these heavy capital intensive industries (those that have more buildings and machines than labour), **or**
b Draw a sketch map to show the shape of the estuary and the location of the industries.

3 a Why is the gas-burning power station near Wilton more environmentally friendly than older coal-burning stations?
b How is ICI dealing with the waste from the manufacture of sulphuric acid?
c How are the brine sites being managed? In what ways are the sites better after development than before?

4 Design an advertisement for the Teesside Development Corporation. Include all the reasons why new companies should come to Teesside and emphasise reliable water supplies.

5 Look at the satellite image (Figure H) which covers Teesside and the surrounding areas. Link up the image with an atlas map of the area. Describe the pattern of major land uses shown on the image.

6 Write viewpoints about the Kielder Reservoir for the following people.
- The Managing Director of Samsung
- An officer with Teesside Development Corporation
- A local villager of Falstone who was re-housed when the reservoir was built
- A member of the Kielder Sailing Club

7 Write about the facilities available at the Kielder Reservoir in a style suitable for a leaflet that can be given away at Tourist Information Points in the surrounding area.

Review

The economy of Teesside has undergone great changes. Local resources are still important for industries and they are being better managed than in the past. The Kielder Scheme despite its original environmental impact has brought benefits as far away as Teesside.

Tourism and leisure

Key ideas

● Tourism and leisure are important to the economy but both can have impacts on the environment.
● Blackpool is Britain's largest seaside resort, with attractions based on natural and people-made resources.

Main activity

This exercise has data response questions and involves planning a visitors' brochure for Blackpool.

The number of visitors who enjoy the countryside and 'wildscape' areas of the UK has remained steady over the past few years. On the other hand visitors to indoor or built leisure facilities have increased (Figure A). The UK's top tourist attractions, or tourist 'magnets', are buildings.

Of the country's top attractions, 60% reported an increase in visitors in 1996. Nearly one in five visitors came from abroad. This is an example of invisible export earnings (see the Language of Trade, page 94). New and old types of leisure facilities flourished in the 1990s, and included industrial heritage sites, old workplaces, steam railways, farm visitor centres, wildlife attractions, gardens and historic houses. New shopping malls also attracted visitors not only for the shops on offer but also for the range of other attractions (see Meadowhall, page 88).

Compared to many economic activities, leisure and tourism do not cause widespread ecological damage. There are, however, important environmental issues to consider (Figure B) These issues are balanced by arguments in favour of leisure and tourism (Figure C).

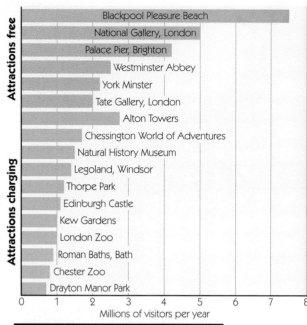

Figure A: The UK's top tourist attractions

Economic It creates employment. There was a 23% increase in employment in the Exmoor National Park 1980–1990 because of tourism. Tourists spend money in a tourist area.

Environmental Many organisations exist to help conserve the countryside.

Amenities Income from visitors can help support local services and industries. Bus services in the Exmoor National Park are kept running by visitor demand.

Figure C: Some of the arguments for tourism

Traffic congestion traffic fumes

Wildlife disturbance

Damage to fragile environments

Conflicts of land use disruption to local residents

The potential environmental impact of leisure and tourism

Loss of 'wilderness' experience (as more development takes place)

Loss of rural culture

Litter/ vandalism

Wear and tear of the countryside and coast

Figure B: The potential environmental impact of leisure and tourism

▼ Questions

1 What types of place are the UK's top tourist attractions?
2 Why is tourism an advantage to many areas of the UK?
3 In what ways can tourism harm rural environments?

CASE STUDY: Blackpool – a seaside resort

The biggest and most popular seaside resort in the United Kingdom is Blackpool in north west England. About 17 million people visit the town each year and 30,000 jobs there depend on tourism. Blackpool was popular with visitors in the 1720s, but it grew as a Victorian seaside resort after the railway arrived in 1846. Its fresh air, sea, beaches and varied amenities provided relaxation and entertainment for the factory workers from northern English cities, e.g. Manchester, Liverpool and Blackburn. Today it is linked to the motorway network which brings 10 million people within 90 minutes' drive of Blackpool. Visitors also come from further afield (Figure D).

The town developed along the coast with the largest hotels at the centre. The many terraced houses and boarding houses make Blackpool one of the most densely populated towns in Britain. Most visitors are day-trippers or on 'short breaks'. One of Blackpool's main attractions is the Pleasure Beach, a large funfair area. There is also the Pepsi Max roller coaster, the Tower, the illuminations, parks and gardens, shops, shows and restaurants. Several conference centres have been established to attract visitors outside the peak holiday season. The successful tourist economy in Blackpool is a result of careful planning and management by the local council and the enterprise of private companies.

- 29,000 jobs provided directly and indirectly for tourism
- Visitors spend £545 million per year
- Over 110 conferences each year attracting 250,000 delegates

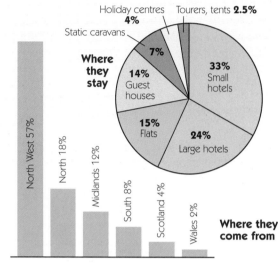

Where they stay

- Holiday centres 4%
- Tourers, tents **2.5%**
- Static caravans 7%
- 14% Guest houses
- 33% Small hotels
- 15% Flats
- 24% Large hotels

Where they come from

- North West 57%
- North 18%
- Midlands 12%
- South 8%
- Scotland 4%
- Wales 2%

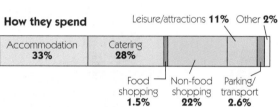

How they spend

| Accommodation 33% | Catering 28% | Food shopping 1.5% | Non-food shopping 22% | Parking/transport 2.6% | Leisure/attractions **11%** | Other **2%** |

Figure D: Facts and figures on Blackpool

Figure E: A Blackpool tram

▼ Questions

4 Where is Blackpool?
5 Why did it grow?
6 Who visited the resort after it grew?
7 Who visits the resort today and what for?
8 Summarise the statistics in Figure D.
9 Blackpool must continue to maintain its attractions, diversify its appeal and advertise itself. Design an outline plan for a future advertising brochure (eight pages) for Blackpool. Think about attracting visitors throughout the year to a range of different attractions, about journey times, and the length of stay for visitors. Include conferences, exhibitions, special events such as concerts, pantomimes and indoor sports events.
You do not have to complete the brochure, only plan one. ➡

Review

Tourism is an important part of the British economy. It has to be planned and managed in order for it not to harm the environment.

Leisure and tourism in Exmoor

In 1954 the Exmoor National Park was set up. Since then, the National Park Authority has managed both leisure and the environment in the Park. This case study is in the form of an enquiry.

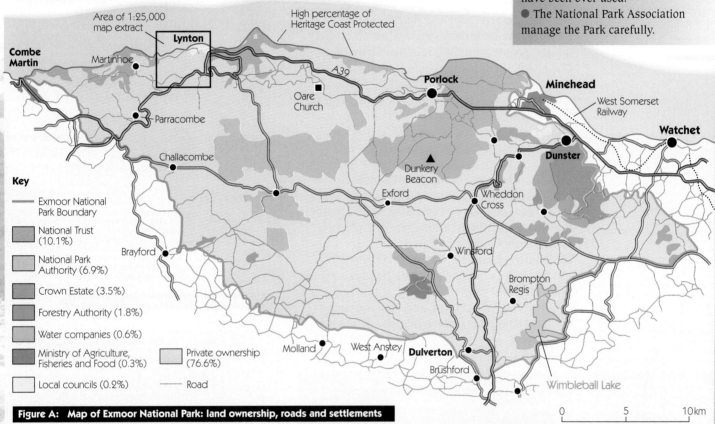

Figure A: Map of Exmoor National Park: land ownership, roads and settlements

Key
— Exmoor National Park Boundary
National Trust (10.1%)
National Park Authority (6.9%)
Crown Estate (3.5%)
Forestry Authority (1.8%)
Water companies (0.6%)
Ministry of Agriculture, Fisheries and Food (0.3%)
Local councils (0.2%)
Private ownership (76.6%)
— Road

0   5   10km

The Exmoor enquiry

What is the impact of tourism and leisure on the Exmoor environment? How is it being managed?

Aim – to investigate:
● background information about rocks and the landscape, climate, land ownership and land use
● the level of tourism in the Park, where people come from, how long they stay, what activities they follow, where they visit
● the impact of tourist activity on the fragile environments
● how the National Park Authority (NPA) manage tourists and leisure activities.

Methods
● Read about the park from pamphlets
● Visit the Park and talk to the Education Officer and Park Rangers
● Use the 1:25,000 Ordnance Survey Outdoor Leisure Map 9
● Observe sites, take photographs and make sketches of the impact of tourist activities
● If possible talk to tourists about their activities.

Results
The results have been presented in a variety of ways. They relate to the two questions asked. Background information has been kept to a minimum.

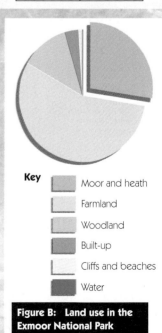

Key
Moor and heath
Farmland
Woodland
Built-up
Cliffs and beaches
Water

Figure B: Land use in the Exmoor National Park

The Background

One of the smaller National Parks in terms of area, Exmoor has a population of under 11,000. The map (Figure A) shows the boundary and land ownership: 71% is in Somerset and 29% in Devon. Average rainfall is over 1800 millimetres on the highest moors but only 1000 millimetres in the east near Minehead and Dunster.

The rocks of Exmoor are sedimentary Devonian and consist of slates, grits and sandstones. The red sandstone soils are well drained. The peaty soils of the highest moors can be very wet. The pie chart (Figure B) shows the Park's land use and the proportion of fragile moorland.

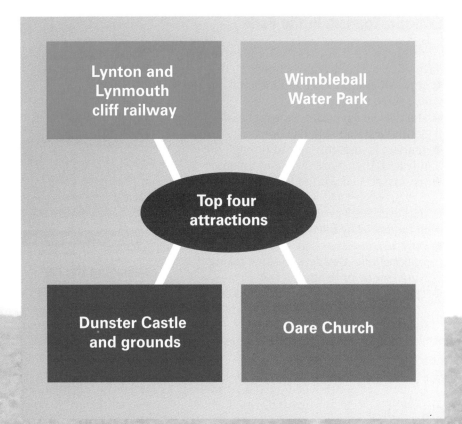

Lynton and Lynmouth cliff railway

Wimbleball Water Park

Top four attractions

Dunster Castle and grounds

Oare Church

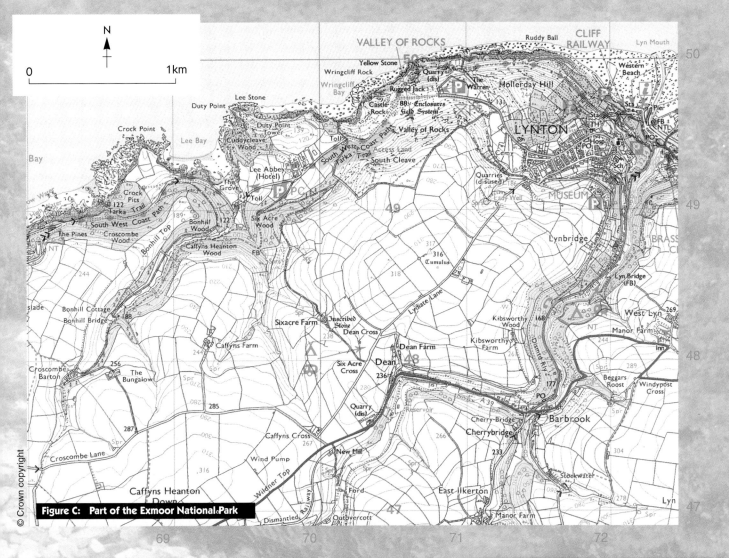

© Crown copyright

Figure C: Part of the Exmoor National Park

Exmoor: Tourism in the Park

There are about two and a half million tourist days spent in the Park every year.

- Most people stay for the traditional one- or two-week holiday.
- Most of the day visitors are on holiday in the South West and visit Exmoor.
- Tourism is unevenly spread through the year; July and August are the busiest months.
- Jobs associated with tourism increased by 23% between 1980 and 1990. It is estimated that over 3000 people are employed directly in tourist related activities.
- Only 20% of visitors are active in terms of walking long distances, cycling, taking part in water sports or fishing.
- There are two long distance footpaths: the northern section of the South West Coast Path follows the Heritage Coast along the coast, and the Two Moors Way which links Dartmoor with Exmoor.
- The highest percentage of visitors come from London and South East England (over 40%).
- Over 90% of visitors arrive by car, the next significant percentage travel by coach.
- There is no main line railway bringing people into the Park but the West Somerset railway has steam trains running into Minehead.

The impact of tourist activity

The car is the biggest problem facing Exmoor. On one day in July 1995, Dunster road traffic came to a standstill. The number of cars in Britain is set to double by 2020 so there are more problems ahead.

- Cyclists, horses and walkers erode the footpaths and wear down the fragile grass and heather moorland.
- Some beauty spots have become too popular and are known as 'honeypots'. There are too many people and cars in too small a place.
- There are many tourist related shops and services in the larger settlements such as Dulverton and Dunster
- The NPA have well used visitor centres at the larger sites.

Figure D: A car parking 'pull-in,' Dunkery Beacon

Managing the car

The NPA have made car parking near moorland paths and bridleways easy; many 'pull-ins' for cars have been cut out (Figure D). Car parking signs are clear; earth humps and strategically placed large stones stop cars parking off the road. Several places have larger car parks with toilets, picnic areas and litter bins (see the OS extract, Figure C). Some of these have been located deliberately to attract tourists and to ease the pressure on the 'honeypot 'sites. One well known tourist site is no longer advertised and does not appear in NPA brochures.

Roads have not been widened and there are no new roads in the Park which would attract more traffic. The Park therefore retains its traditional narrow and winding roads with high banks with hedges. The hedges are well maintained using available grants.

There is no Park and Ride scheme but there is a subsidised visitor bus which completes three loops of the Park a day, and is being widely advertised. One bus (Figure E) linking Lynmouth to Dulverton was empty on a warm Friday in late July – this was the 2.30 p.m. departure from Dulverton.

Figure E: The Red Bus linking Lynmouth with Dulverton

Figure F: Off-road cyclists near Dunkery Beacon

Figure H: The Dunkery Project to maintain footpaths

Managing the Rights of Way

Exmoor is popular with walkers, horse riders and off-road cyclists (Figure F). Well used rights of way cross the Dunkery Beacon area, the highest point in Exmoor at 519 metres. The fieldsketch (Figure G) is from the area of Dunkery Beacon and shows footpath management techniques such as waterlets and boulder placement. This work to maintain the footpaths is part of the Dunkery Project (Figure H). It employs two footpath technicians who, in turn, use volunteers for the labour intensive work. The Project is funded by the NPA, the National Trust and the Countryside Commission. In the future, there may be EC funding for footpath management; in the meantime there is European funding for a new 'green brochure' which will help educate visitors about the need to manage the fragile Exmoor environments.

Footpaths on the urban fringe also need managing. Near Minehead Youth Hostel, silver birch chippings are used to cover footpaths. The silver birch has to be cut down anyway as it is invading the heathland. A wood chipper has been bought and children spread the chippings on footpaths when they are wet. The children are given gloves for the simple job. It is an example of using local materials at low cost to sustain a well used footpath on the edge of a built-up area.

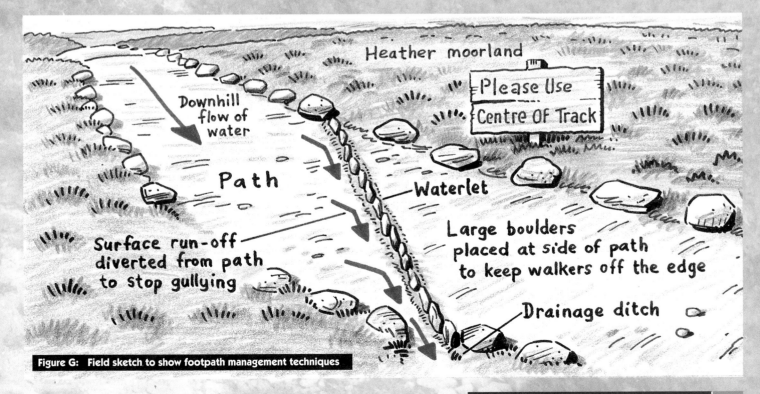

Figure G: Field sketch to show footpath management techniques

maintaining the traditional natural environment and to provide facilities for the visitors. The illustrations show the efforts being made to direct the tourists to car parks and to the existing rights of way.

Footpath technicians are preventing future wear and tear of the fragile moorland. Gullies in the paths are made by the high water run-off after high rainfall. Building **waterlets** is a key method of erosion control. It is important to subtly persuade the walkers to use the footpaths so as to avoid erosion.

Providing new locations for tourists suggests to them that they do not have to go to the well known sites. Educating the visitors using Rangers and an Education Officer, through visitor centres and well produced pamphlets, appear to be important.

Promoting bus travel and subsidising the Visitor Bus is a step towards persuading tourists to leave their cars.

Analysis

The impact of tourism and leisure on the Exmoor environment is greatest in the larger settlements where there are visitor centres and many tourist related shops and services. The narrow roads in Exmoor are a problem at busy times. Car parks and pull-ins are very well used especially in the middle of the day. There is a significant number of tourists from Europe, including Germans and Dutch. On a warm summer's day people of a wide age range walk and cycle, picnic and enjoy sightseeing. Many people appear to be near their cars but this was not studied in any detail. The impact of tourism can be seen on employment, but those jobs directly related to tourism are very seasonal.

The NPA use their limited powers to plan and manage tourism. Grants are available for

Conclusion and limitations

The impact of tourism can be seen in the settlements of Exmoor and in the employment statistics. The harmful impacts concern the environment; they involve the increasing number of cars and the damage to the rights of way and the moorland that lies beside them. Surface run-off can quickly make gullies in a well used path or bridleway.

Tourists can be encouraged to park their cars where the planners want them to. They can also be directed away from traditional 'honeypots'. Moorland paths can be successfully improved and maintained using waterlets and other techniques. Signposts which are not obtrusive in the landscape can inform and direct the tourists.

The NPA planners need environmental protection laws to manage the tourists e.g. the Heritage Coast, the Environmentally Sensitive Area, the SSSI, the National Nature Reserve and the National Park. Funding the environment and subsidising activities is essential; this comes from a variety of sources including Europe. Educating the tourists is very important.

The future for Exmoor would seem to be one where the growth of the car is limited. An increase in **public transport** will have to be encouraged. Initiatives such as the Dunkery Project are needed and funding from Europe would be helpful. The moorland needs to be sustained and even improved. The effects of tourism need to be balanced with the needs of the local people and the conservation of the environment. Green tourism, which is environmentally friendly, should be encouraged.

This enquiry set out to answer two questions. This limited the scope of the enquiry as environmental management and conservation involve more than just tourism. Only a limited number of areas were visited and the coastal areas were left out. Two useful further areas of study would be footpath use and car parking. More formal questionnaires could be used to interview tourists about their activities; this would need to be done sensitively to avoid being intrusive. Further work could be done on heathland management, farming and woodland conservation.

▼ Questions

1 Study the extract from the Ordnance Survey 1:25,000 Outdoor Leisure Map, Number 9 (Figure C).
   a What is the six figure grid reference of the youth hostel in the river valley south of Lynton?
   b How far is it from the youth hostel (in a straight line) to the beach at Wringcliffe Bay, in the north west of the extract?
   c What extra detail does this scale of map show compared to the 1:50,000 OS map?
   d List all the map evidence for tourism and leisure activities.
   e Describe the coastal scenery you might see if you walked along the Coastal Path from east to west.

2 Find the very small building on the field boundary at grid reference 698476. This used to be a cricket pavilion and the land had at one time been in sports use. The landowner applied for planning permission to turn five fields to the west of it into a golf course (about 40 hectares or 100 acres). The NPA were totally against the plans and opposed them in a public enquiry. State the possible arguments for and against the plans for the golf course.

3 There is interest in developing the dismantled railway which can be seen on the map. In what ways could this type of land be used? Who would benefit from the developments you describe?

4 At Whitechapel Moors near South Moulton just outside the Park boundary there has been a planning application for a very large holiday development. There would be good access by the main A361(T) road. The development would affect the National Park. Suggest how the following organisations and people reacted to the proposals.

   The National Park Authority, Devon County Council, the local farmer who owns the land, the young people of the nearby farms and villages, the Campaign for the Protection of Rural England, the Holiday Development Company. (A class could use this as a role play exercise and more roles could be included.)

5 Further work on the enquiry.
   Study the field sketch (Figure G) of footpath management near Dunkery Beacon. Write in detail about how the paths are being maintained and improved. How can the tourists be guided to use the paths properly? ➡

6 Write your own summary answers to the enquiry questions written at the beginning of the enquiry. ➡

7 Write a plan for an enquiry that you would like to undertake in the Exmoor National Park. Ask simple questions that it is possible to answer. Use the enquiry method described in this chapter.

Review

The pressure of tourists and their cars in Exmoor is being managed by the NPA. Cars are directed to planned car parks and away from areas under pressure. Rights of way are being improved by building waterlets and the tourists are being encouraged to use all paths carefully.

3 The changing economy

Main activity

The main activity in this exercising is summarising reasons for economic change and defining economic terms.

Key ideas

● The structure of employment changed in the UK during the period of de-industrialisation.
● Specialisation is not as important in UK regions as it was.
● Some regions are being revitalised by government incentives and inward foreign investment.

Key	%
1 East Midlands	35.39
2 West Midlands	34.33
3 North	31.33
4 Wales	30.18
5 Yorks and Humber	30.04
6 North-west	29.57
7 East Anglia	27.39
8 Scotland	26.23
9 Northern Ireland	26.11
10 South-west	25.79
11 South-east	22.04

WORKSHOP OF THE WORLD HAS PUT UP THE SHUTTERS

Britain has only two representatives in the European Union top 20 of manufacturing regions, according to research. There was a time when Britain was the workshop of the world, and the West Midlands was the workshop of Britain. Now the West Midlands just scrapes into the top 20.

Adapted from the *Guardian*, 31 Dec 1996

This unit of the book is titled Economic Activity, and in this unit you will be able to study the changes in the UK economy through case studies. The overall changes in the economy will be described and explained. There are case studies of a farm, the aluminium industry, a car factory and an industrial estate. Two regional studies will help you see that the economic geography of the UK is less specialised than it used to be.

During the last decades of the twentieth century coal mining and manufacturing industry declined. The process became known as **de-industrialisation**. Alongside de-industrialisation was the continued movement of workers away from farming. The three pie graphs (Figure A) summarise the changes in employment structure since 1961. Compare these with the stages of development countries pass through. The United Kingdom has become a **post-industrial economy** (Figure B). Figure C gives information about manufacturing in the UK regions. Figure D gives some explanations for the changes in the UK economy.

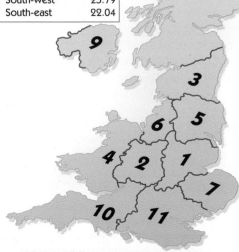

Figure C: Manufacturing in the UK regions

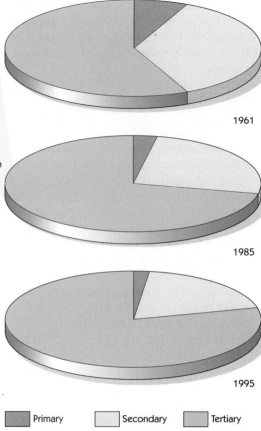

1961

1985

1995

| ▨ Primary | ▢ Secondary | ▦ Tertiary |

Figure A: Britain's changing structure of employment

Figure B: The stages of development through which countries pass

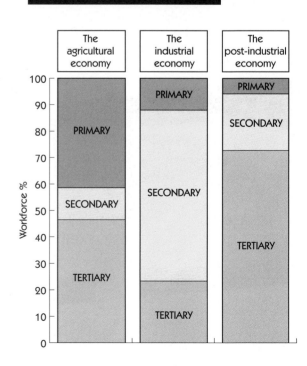

COAL FROM NEWCASTLE

In 1901 one in four workers in Durham –100,000 men – worked under ground in coal-mines. By March next year the figure will be close to zero. All four of the pits in Durham and Tyne-and-Wear will close. The oldest coalfield in the world will have died. Were it not for the survival of Ellington (thanks to its local customer, Alcan, which smelts aluminium at Lynemouth), mining in the north-east would all but vanish.

The Economist,
17 Oct 1992

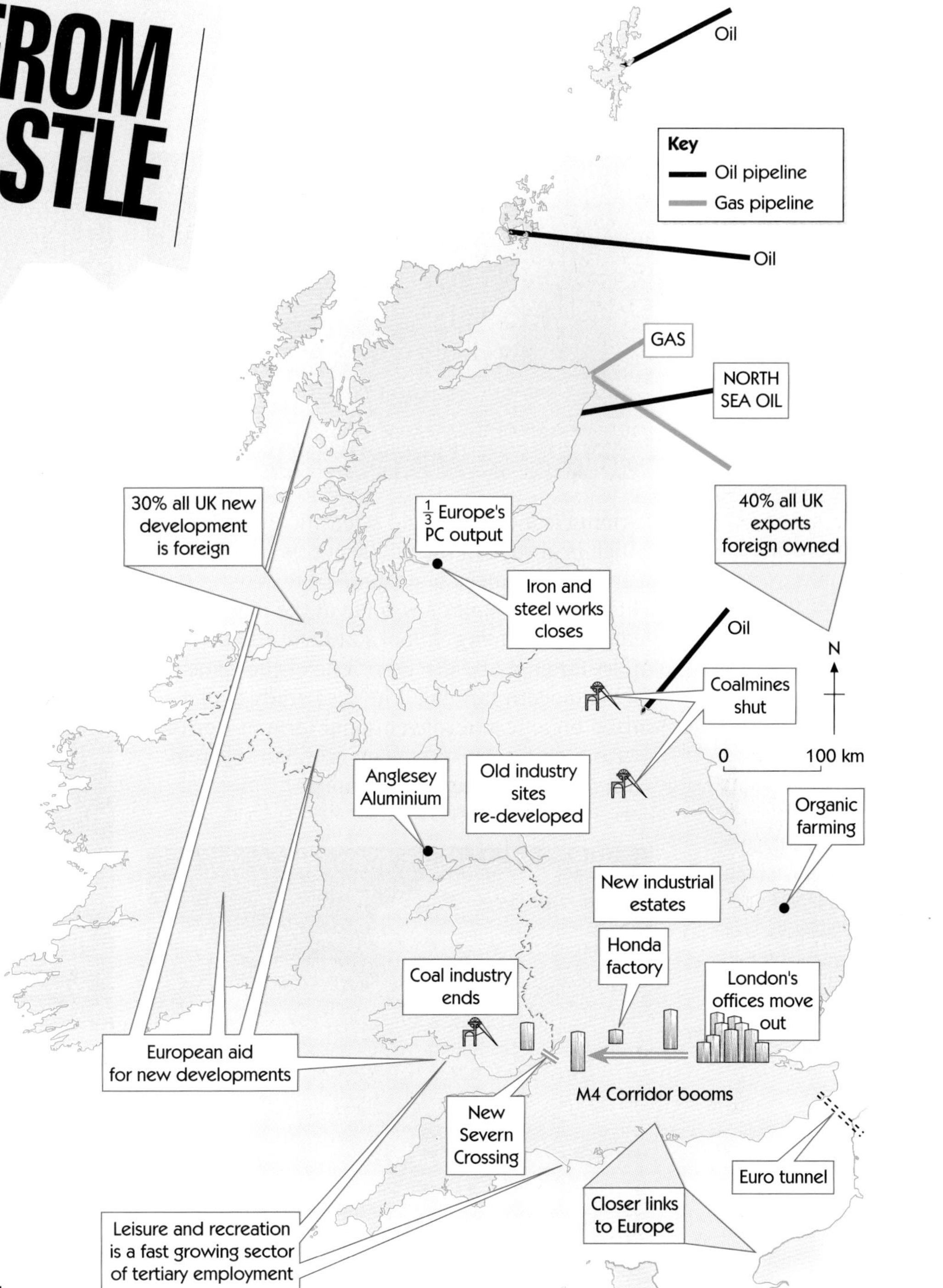

Oil

Key
— Oil pipeline
— Gas pipeline

Oil

GAS

NORTH SEA OIL

30% all UK new development is foreign

⅓ Europe's PC output

40% all UK exports foreign owned

Iron and steel works closes

Oil

Coalmines shut

N

0   100 km

Anglesey Aluminium

Old industry sites re-developed

Organic farming

New industrial estates

Honda factory

London's offices move out

Coal industry ends

European aid for new developments

M4 Corridor booms

New Severn Crossing

Euro tunnel

Closer links to Europe

Leisure and recreation is a fast growing sector of tertiary employment

Figure D: The UK's changing economy

▼ Questions

1 What do you understand by the terms primary, secondary and tertiary industries?

2 Explain what is meant by the following economic terms:
   a de-industrialisation
   b heavy industry
   c footloose industries
   d an industrial region
   e specilisation.

3 Summarise the changing economy of the United Kingdom under the following headings. For each heading, write one or two lines stating what has happened and why.
   a Workers are leaving farming
   b Coalmines have closed
   c The traditional regions are being revitalised
   d Offices are moving out of London and other city centres
   e There are closer links with Europe

Review

Traditional industries and specialised industrial regions have disappeared. New manufacturing and office developments are more footloose and are influenced by political policies and foreign investors.

Farming

In this exercise students can design a questionnaire that could be used to investigate a large mixed farm.

Key ideas

● Farms are economic systems that have inputs, processes and outputs.

● Farming varies within the UK because it is influenced by physical, economic and political factors.

● Intensive farming has produced a reliable food supply but there have been environmental and health costs.

● Organic farming and non-food farming are increasing.

> **Fertilisers are necessary if enough food is to be grown to feed the world's increasing population.**
>
> **Society has to decide on its priorities. How will it balance cheap, efficiently produced, high quality food with concern about water quality and the countryside?**
>
> *The Fertiliser Manufacturers Association*

Farming is a complex and scientific industry which is always in the public eye. It also has to respond to changes in demand from consumers. This spread summarises some of the main features of farming. It looks at factors that affect farming and discusses one of the issues facing modern farming. The case study is of a mixed organic and conventional farm in Norfolk.

Farming can be seen as an economic system with inputs and outputs (Figure C).

Figure B: Sacks of Nitrogen and Sulphur fertiliser made by ICI at Billingham on Teesside for use on conventional, intensive farms. The nitrates washed off farmland have polluted rivers especially in arable farming areas

> **We are launching a national campaign demanding a change in government food and farming policies to help turn Britain organic.**
>
> *The Soil Association*

Figure A: Organic carrots packed for a supermarket chain. These were grown in Norfolk without fertilisers or insecticides

Do you know?

Since the UK joined The European Economic Community in 1973 (now the EU) farming has been affected by the Common Agricultural Policy (CAP).

Its aims have been to:

? increase productivity and therefore reduce imports

? ensure employment and a fair standard of living for farmers

? safeguard prices and supplies

? make marketing easier

Some results of CAP have been to:

? pay farmers above world prices and at the same time stop cheap imports

? reduce dairy herds because of over production of milk

? increase the production of oil seed rape

? increase the number of sheep in the UK

? produce surpluses such as the 'butter mountain'

? bring in 'set-aside' for arable land (land taken out of production)

Inputs →	Processes →	Outputs →	Markets
Rock/Soil type	Ploughing	Cash crops	Pick Your Own
Climate	Planting	Fodder crops	Farm shop
Hazards	Weeding	Non-food crops	Local
Relief and slope	Spraying	Meat	National
Plants	Irrigating	Live animals	Exports
Seeds	Harvesting	Dairy products	Contracts
Animals	Calving/Lambing	Eggs	Canning
Fertiliser	Research	Forest products	Freezing
Pesticides	Building	Flowers	European surplus
Machinery	Fencing	Other - Camping	Food aid
Investment in buildings	Keeping accounts	Education	Non-food industry
Leisure			

Figure C: Farming as an input/output system

What affects the choice of farming?

Every farmer will be influenced by **physical factors** such as the height of land, the slopes, the direction the slopes face, rainfall, temperatures, sunshine and natural hazards such as drought and flood. **Economic factors** such as the availability of money or bank loans and the price of inputs will also be important. Farmers will have their own particular interests and will want to experiment with new ideas. **Government policies** (including the European Union Common Agricultural Policy) will also affect what farmers do. Finally the **demand** from consumers is important; this alters with changing wealth, tastes and responses to health scares, healthy eating campaigns and advertising.

Farming methods and the future

The quotations at the beginning and the two photographs (Figures A and B) illustrate the choices facing farming. How can the nation continue to produce food as cheaply as possible and at the same time protect both the environment and people's long term health? People want good quality food that looks goods, tastes good and is cheap. They want to avoid food scares such as salmonella in eggs, BSE in beef, genetically engineered fruits and *E. coli* in meats. People also want rivers free of farm pollutants and the countryside with its hedgerows and wildlife.

The farmers' point of view is that they need to be able to make a profit farming. Farmers today do not have to farm more land or even to farm more intensively, as there is enough of certain foods in the UK and Europe (cereal surpluses and butter mountains). Some farmers have chosen to change their farming methods and their land use.

Roves Farm

At Roves Farm in north east Wiltshire, farmer Mr Burr has diversified from sheep rearing. He now grows willow trees which fuel a small electricity generator. The farmer has also planted a hay meadow with traditional grasses and wild flowers using no chemical fertilisers or insecticides. A wetland has been established and a variety of trees planted. The Farm Visitor Centre specialises in lambing, which visitors can see for several weeks in the spring. Because the ewes are artificially inseminated the lambing period can be planned this way. Meanwhile the traditional farming activities still continue; about 1500 lambs are sold to Europe each year and the crops of wheat and barley are sold locally.

▼ Question

Design a questionnaire which would help you find out about a farm and its outputs. It should have questions which are concerned with recent changes in methods and farm diversification. At least 20 questions will be needed.

Review

Farming is an economic system which is affected by a variety of factors. Political decisions lead to individual farmers making decisions about farming methods and land use.

CASE STUDY: An organic farm in East Anglia

Key ideas

● East Anglia has physical and economic advantages for large scale arable farming.

● Bagthorpe Farm in Norfolk is 50% organic and is an example of what farms may be like in the future.

Main activity

In this activity students ask questions in depth about conventional and organic farming, and practice decision making.

The UK's most important farming region

The location of the East Anglian region is shown in Figure A, while Figure B shows some of its soil types. It is the country's most important farming region but only a small percentage of the region's population is employed in farming. This is because the agriculture is highly **intensive** and **commercial**. Machines and computers do the work and only a minimum number of people are needed.

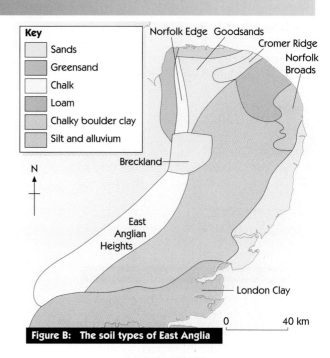

Key
- Sands
- Greensand
- Chalk
- Loam
- Chalky boulder clay
- Silt and alluvium

Figure B: The soil types of East Anglia

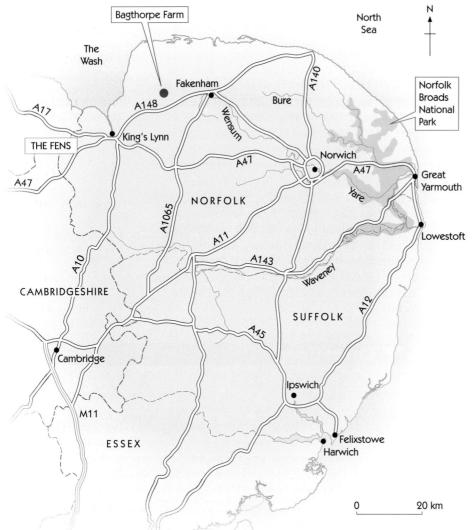

Figure A: East Anglia: Norfolk and Suffolk. The East Anglia planning region also includes Cambridgeshire

Physical advantages

● Summers are warm: July 15°– 16°C and sunny with 6.5 hours per day in July
● Winters are cold: January 4°– 5°C with hard frosts
● Rainfall is low: under 700 mm but mostly it is in the growing season
● Soils are varied and can be used selectively for different crops
● Much of the land is flat or undulating and is suited to large machines

Economic advantages

● Close to large markets of London and the West Midlands
● A long history of farming enterprise and innovation
● Farms are large and efficient, many over 200 hectares
● Farms are often owned by large companies and are run as 'agri-businesses' which specialise for **contract** farming

Organic farming at Bagthorpe Farm

Bagthorpe Farm is in north Norfolk to the north of the Kings Lynn to Fakenham road (Figure A). The farm lies between 50 and 70 metres above sea level, and had been recommended as good example of a modern organic farm. Before visiting the farm, a questionnaire was prepared and sent to the farmer, Mr Morton. Below are the replies to the questionnaire. Sometimes extra questions were needed to gain a full understanding of the farm business.

Questionnaire

1 What is the size of the farm?
240 hectares/600 acres. It is a continuous area.

2 What is the ownership situation?
Private ownership.

3 Is there any recent history of the farm in terms of size and ownership?
There is a map of the farm in 1830 and the size and shape today is the same. There has been a farm here since Saxon times – *thorpe* is a Saxon daughter settlement.

4 What is the rock/soil coverage?
Well below ground beyond root depth is chalk. The covering soil is a mix of glacial sands and gravels.

5 Is there a water problem?
It is a low rainfall area and it is necessary to spray irrigate.

6 What crops are grown?
The map (Figure C) shows all the crops. About half is conventional farming and the other half is organic farming (see Figures D to G). The yields for the organic crops are usually lower.

7 What animals are kept?
35 cows and 1 bull and their calves. This is for beef. This herd will be replaced and the next one will be organic. 105 sows and their litters. Some lambs kept in the winter for fattening and grazing the ley grasses.

8 What is the farm labour situation?
The farmer, 3 full time workers and 1 man who shares the pig business with the farmer. 6 regular part time workers and up to 20 locally based seasonal workers.

9 What are the most important machines and buildings/stores?
6 tractors, 1 combine harvester, separate harvesters which fix to the tractors for potatoes, carrots and onions (Figure H). A soil separator, mechanical hoes, a sprayer and a loader. 6 large dry store sheds for onions and grass seed.

10 What are the main markets, in terms of the main outputs?
The organic potatoes go to Waitrose supermarkets. The organic onions go to an organic wholesaler in West Wales. The spelt wheat goes to a specialist mill in Hungerford. The strawberries go to Yeovil. The markets vary according to who wants to buy the crop.

11 What other income comes from the farm?
Only some wood sales.

12 Why is the farm organic?
(See Figure I which summarises the conversation with Mr Morton.)

13 What did you have to do to become organic?
It took about 3 years to prepare. No sprays or inorganic fertilisers could be used on the selected fields. Fertility had to be built up using nitrogen fixing clover leys. Pigs and cattle were also grazed on the fields to provide organic manure.

14 What do you have to do to maintain the organic standards?
Keep to a non-exploitive and fertility building rotation. A 9 year rotation is maintained (Figure J).

15 What financial assistance is there from the British Government?
Very little help for organic farming but a conversion scheme for farmers who are new to organic farming.

16 What financial assistance is there from the European Union?
There is the general assistance from the CAP.

17 What environmental issues are there on the farm?
The hedgerows lost in the past have not been replaced. Bird numbers have fallen recently especially skylarks, thrushes and swallows.

18 What environmental improvements have you made?
3 woods have been planted with the help of government grants. Some pheasants have been introduced.

19 What other areas of concern are there to do with the farm?
There are 10 farm cottages close to the farm and at present they are all lived in and there are no holiday homes; I hope it remains like this.

20 How much organic farming is there in this country and in Europe?
In the mid 1990s there was only 0.3% of land in Britain under organic production. This should reach 1% by 2000. This is well behind some EU countries where 10% is the target for 2000.

Do you know?

? Some key words for farming

arable   crop farming

permanent pasture   grassland

ley grass   a temporary crop of grass

yield   the amount produced for a given area or animal

intensive   where there are a lot of inputs and a high output

extensive   where there are few inputs and the output is low

contracts   an agreement between a farmer and a food processing company e.g. a farmer will contract to grow peas for Birds Eye

inorganic (artificial) fertiliser   one containing manufactured chemicals such as nitrogen, phosphorous, potassium and sulphur

organic fertiliser   naturally occuring nutrients in the form of manure, animal waste, plant remains

nitrogen fixing   the process of nitrogen being passed from the roots of plants into the soils. Clover and other legumes such as beans fix nitrogen.

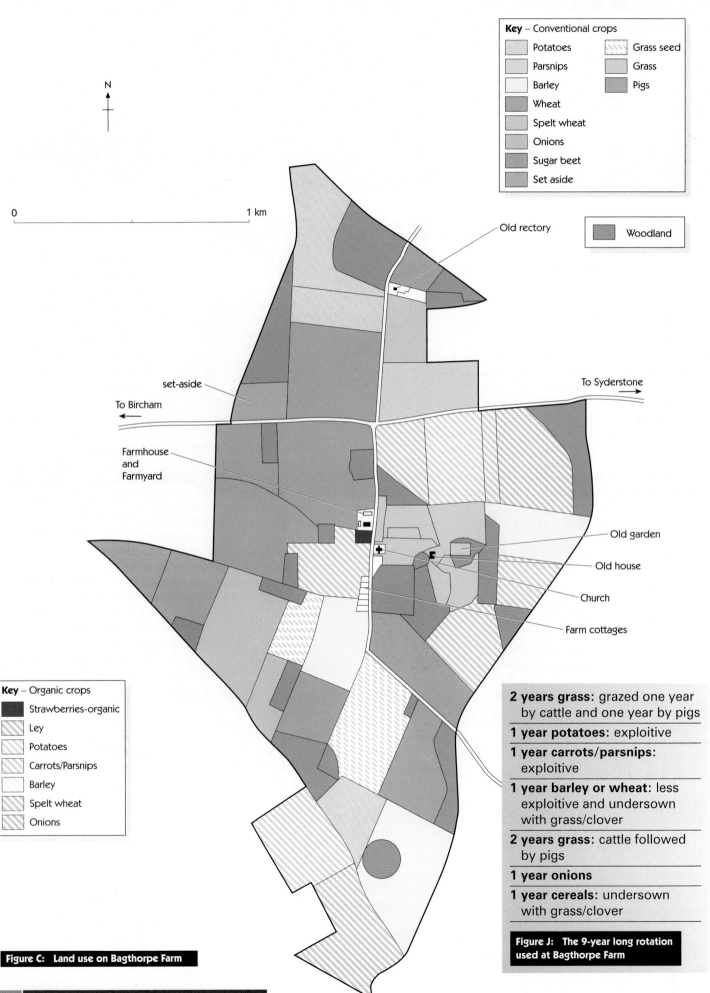

Key – Conventional crops

- Potatoes
- Parsnips
- Barley
- Wheat
- Spelt wheat
- Onions
- Sugar beet
- Set aside
- Grass seed
- Grass
- Pigs

Woodland

Old rectory

set-aside

To Syderstone

To Bircham

Farmhouse and Farmyard

Old garden

Old house

Church

Farm cottages

Key – Organic crops

- Strawberries-organic
- Ley
- Potatoes
- Carrots/Parsnips
- Barley
- Spelt wheat
- Onions

2 years grass: grazed one year by cattle and one year by pigs

1 year potatoes: exploitive

1 year carrots/parsnips: exploitive

1 year barley or wheat: less exploitive and undersown with grass/clover

2 years grass: cattle followed by pigs

1 year onions

1 year cereals: undersown with grass/clover

Figure J: The 9-year long rotation used at Bagthorpe Farm

Figure C: Land use on Bagthorpe Farm

Figure D: Organic potatoes

Figure E: Organic onions

Figure F: Organic barley

Figure G: Organic carrots

Figure H: The farm's combine harvester with a potato harvester in the foreground

Figure D shows organic potatoes in the field to the north east of the farm with the ley field in the background. The tractor is fitted with a cutter that trims off the tops of the potato plants. This makes digging the potatoes easier and it also spreads the green tops which will rot down as compost. Note the light sandy soil containing irregular glacial stones. Organic onions (Figure E) grow in the north east of the farm next to the organic barley field. Note the fairly flat land. These onions have been weeded by hand. The organic barley (Figure F) is south of the onion field. Note the spaces between the plants and the abundant weeds. The organic carrots (Figure G) at the southern end of the farm are a high quality and good yielding crop but damaged by rabbits near the edges of the field. In Figure H you can see the farm's combine harvester with a potato harvester in the foreground. To the right are two vegetable harvesters. Behind is a truck, a roller and a plough. In the background are the dry stores with the empty wooden potato bins stacked up.

Questions

1 Write a definition of organic farming and state how organic farming can be set up and maintained.
2 How many 'organic' fields has Mr Morton? Use the land use map, Figure C.
3 Which crops are grown conventionally but not organically?
4 Draw up a systems diagram for the organic crops grown on the farm. Follow the example in Figure C, page 49. You will need the details of the organic processes such as rotation, clover leys and cattle grazing. Include the markets for the individual crops.
5 What are the advantages and disadvantages of conventional farming compared to organic farming?
6 Draw up a plan for organic farming on the land north of the Bircham to Syderstone road. Draw a map to show your land use after three years of establishing the organic farming methods. You can plan to grow more than one crop within the present field boundaries.

Why organic?

- I began to think about conventional farming after the bumper harvest of 1984.
- Some of the surplus crops were being stored and some dumped on the world markets reducing the prices for farmers everywhere.
- There was an increasing risk to the environment from the chemical farming methods.
- There were some health scares and people were beginning to question the ethics of such large scale farming.
- Many workers could not find work on the highly mechanised farms and it seemed wrong that they lived in the countryside but could not work in it.
- Organic farming would provide jobs for local people.
- Organic farming would be more in balance with the local environment.
- There was a growing demand for organic food and the market outlets were opening up.

Figure I: Why Mr Morton chose organic farming

Review

East Anglia has developed as a highly commercial and intensive farming region. Bagthorpe Farm is an example of an alternative approach to profitable farming.

Manufacturing and industry

The information on this spread will help you understand why secondary industries locate in particular places. Read about each example and then answer the questions about it.

Oil refining and petrochemicals on Teesside

The North Tees oil refinery is on the north bank of the River Tees and occupies a large site (Figure A). It is built on land reclaimed from the river estuary (see the satellite image, Figure H, page 37). The refinery receives crude oil by pipeline from the North Sea as well as by oil tankers from other oilfields. The chemical works on the same site produces raw materials (feedstock) for making a wide range of fibres, textiles, plastics and paint. Some products are shipped out of the Tees and some are sent by pipeline to Billingham and Wilton.

Iron and steel in Motherwell

There was a long history of making iron and steel in the Motherwell area of Lanarkshire, central Scotland. In the nineteenth century coal and iron ore were mined alongside each other. Iron ore was later imported, and steel scrap came from the shipbuilding areas of Clydeside. By 1963 a new iron and steel works, with a strip mill, had been completed at Ravenscraig in Motherwell. It employed 9000 workers, as part of Government Regional Policy to build up industry in declining regions. A car factory and a truck plant were built close by, and both used steel from Ravenscraig.

In 1992 the steel works shut down and there began a spiral of decline (Figure B). Firms which relied on Ravenscraig lost money or went out of business, and £45 million of wages were lost. The decline was devastating. Some new developments have since taken place and reversed the downward spiral:

● Motherwell was made an Enterprise Zone to attract inward investment
● The European Union funded training schemes for redundant steelworkers
● The Scottish freight terminal for Eurotunnel was built there
● The Lanarkshire Development Agency has attracted firms.

Figure B: The spiral of decline

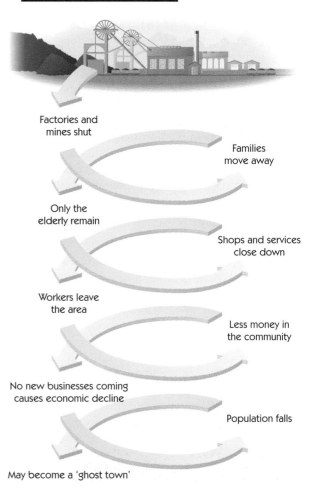

Factories and mines shut

Families move away

Only the elderly remain

Shops and services close down

Workers leave the area

Less money in the community

No new businesses coming causes economic decline

Population falls

May become a 'ghost town'

Figure A: The site of the North Tees Works looking north east

TV tubes and computer monitors in Scotland

Since the closure of the Ravenscraig steel works, the Taiwanese television tube manufacturer Chunghwa has built a factory employing 3000 people. In 1996 there was more success for Lanarkshire (see Figure C).

Such investment by **footloose** high-tech companies can start a cycle of wealth. This is the opposite to a spiral of decline. Once an area develops industry it will continue to attract other companies. Service and component industries develop and the area gains a reputation. This is called the multiplier effect and was first described by the economist Gunnar Myrdal; Figure D is a diagram of this model of growth. Since the beginning of the 1990s the UK has done better than other major manufacturing countries in terms of output per person (Figure E). This success, and the fact that there are low labour costs, has attracted foreign investment (also see South Wales, page 62).

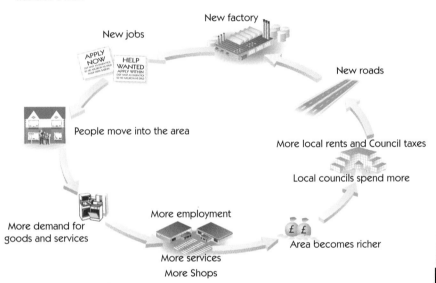

Figure D: The model of growth, adapted from Myrdal's model

New factory
New jobs
New roads
People move into the area
More local rents and Council taxes
Local councils spend more
More demand for goods and services
Area becomes richer
More employment
More services
More Shops

TAIWANESE IN £40M SCOTS VENTURE

A £40m Taiwanese investment in Scotland which will create more than 1000 jobs over the next two years was announced yesterday. The Lite-On Technology Corporation, the world's fifth largest computer monitor manufacturer, has chosen Lanarkshire as the location for its first European manufacturing facility. The Prime Minister said that Scotland was 'one of Europe's most attractive business environments.'

Mr Soong, chairman of Lite-On, said: 'We looked at a number of sites elsewhere in Europe but a combination of factors such as market potential, availability of a skilled workforce and the overall business infrastructure already established in Scotland could not be matched anywhere else.'

Figure C: Taiwanese investment will help establish a new cycle of wealth in Scotland

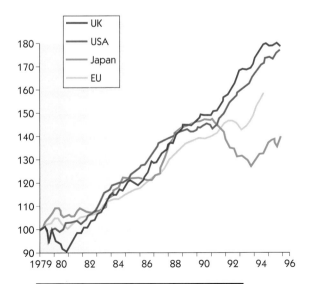

Figure E: UK ouput per person employed in manufacturing

Legend: UK, USA, Japan, EU

▼ Questions

1 Draw a flow diagram of the site advantages and production of oil and chemicals at the North Tees Works. Use the following words:

flat land	crude oil	pipeline	oil tanker
Billingham	Wilton	textiles	plastics
North Sea	feedstock	River Tees	

2 a Explain how the closure of the Motherwell iron and steel works started off a spiral of decline.

  b Explain how the downward spiral is being stopped and reversed.

3 a Why is Scotland seen as an attractive business environment?

  b In what ways will a Taiwanese company be able to start a new cycle of wealth in central Scotland?

Review

The three examples show different location and site factors. The Scottish examples illustrate the spiral of decline and the multiplier effect. Foreign investment has been important in Scotland and in other areas of the UK.

CASE STUDY: The aluminium industry in Britain

Main activity

In this exercise students can follow through the geography of aluminium from the bauxite ore to the foil sweet wrapper or aluminium drinks can.

Key ideas

● Aluminium plants are closely tied to the sources of their raw materials and energy.
● The aluminium product manufacturers are not located in the same place as the aluminium producers.

Making aluminium in Anglesey

There are two small aluminium **smelting** firms in Scotland at Fort William and Kinlochleven. They were located close to **hydro-electric power** sources. There is a large smelter in Northumberland at Lynemouth located next to a coal-fired power station and another at Holyhead in Anglesey, North Wales. The smelter at Holyhead was opened in 1971. Figure B shows the advantages of its location and site. There were over 100 hectares of flat land available; government grants were on offer to help with the building as it was in a Development Area. The smelter uses the same amount of electricity a day as a city of 250,000 people does in a year! The Anglesey works produces 126,000 tonnes of aluminium a year which is transported to the product manufacturers to be made into foil, strip and sheet aluminium.

The company is sensitive to environmental issues. It offers recycling facilities and runs a nearby farm and a coastal nature park. The company brochure states that, 'Plant emissions to the atmosphere are controlled and no CFC or ozone layer depleting substances are used in the plant's processes.'

Aluminium foil from Bridgnorth

Bridgnorth, on the river Severn, is to the west of Birmingham and to the south of Telford. At the Lawson Mardon Star factory aluminium foil is made for sweets, cakes, biscuits and dairy products (Figure A). Next time you unwrap a sweet think about the thickness of the foil – it will be less than 0.1mm. In the UK some 75,000 tonnes of aluminium foil a year is manufactured. Foil has many advantages over other types of packaging. It is flexible, strong, an efficient barrier to light, low in weight and can be recycled.

At the Bridgnorth works, processes include hot and cold rolling, laminating, printing and embossing. Ingots of aluminium are imported from Iceland and the Anglesey Aluminium works. Unlike the smelter, the factory is not tied to sources of bulky raw materials and an energy supply. It is more important that the factory is near a source of skilled labour. It also needs to be linked into the country's transport system to get the products to market.

Recovering aluminium from used products costs only 5% of the cost of making aluminium. There is a target to recycle 10% of foil.

Figure A: Aluminium foil for chocolate and sweet wrappings

Aluminium cans from Wakefield

Europe's largest can manufacturer is Nacanco, whose largest UK plant is at Wakefield in West Yorkshire. The company also make cans at Runcorn and Milton Keynes. Carnaud Metal Box make cans at Carlisle and Leicester and Continental Cans at Wrexham and Rugby. These plants have been located near the labour supplies and the markets.

At Wakefield, drinks cans are made from aluminium strip which is about 0.2mm thick. The strip arrives from the aluminium producers in huge coils and the container is made in two parts – the can and the end. The drinks manufacturers fill the cans and seal on the top ends. Aluminium is now used in 80% of the drinks packaging industry and 8.5 billion cans are made in the UK each year. The aluminium can was only introduced in 1960. The can is totally recyclable and the UK recycling rate was over 30% in 1996 with a target of 50% for 2001 (worldwide, the rate achieved is already 50%).

▼ Questions

1 Where are Britain's four aluminium smetlers?
2 What location factor do the aluminium smelters have in common?
3 What do the smelters have to import?
4 Explain why the following location factors were important for the Anglesey aluminium smelter:
government grants   power   deep sea water
rail and road transport   flat land
5 Why was the foil factory able to locate separately from the aluminium smelter? (Think about transport, markets, labour.)
6 Attempt to draw a flow diagram to show the geography of a sweet wrapper or drinks can. You will need to use line sketches to show the raw materials and different types and transport and locations.

Figure B: The location and site of Anglesey Aluminium

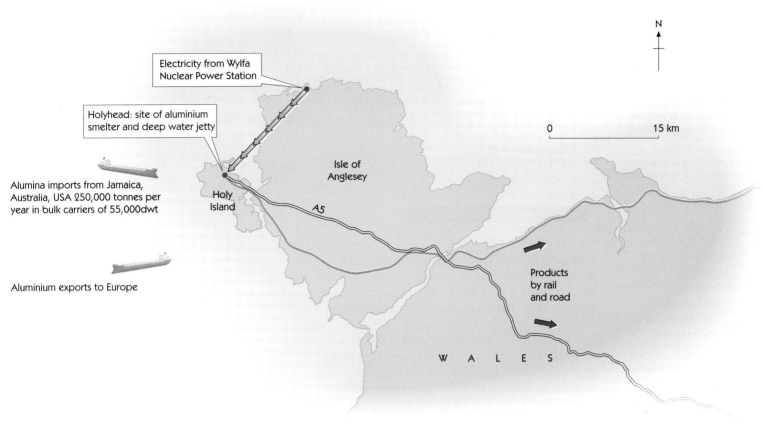

Electricity from Wylfa Nuclear Power Station

Holyhead: site of aluminium smelter and deep water jetty

Alumina imports from Jamaica, Australia, USA 250,000 tonnes per year in bulk carriers of 55,000dwt

Aluminium exports to Europe

Isle of Anglesey

Holy Island

A5

0   15 km

Products by rail and road

W A L E S

N

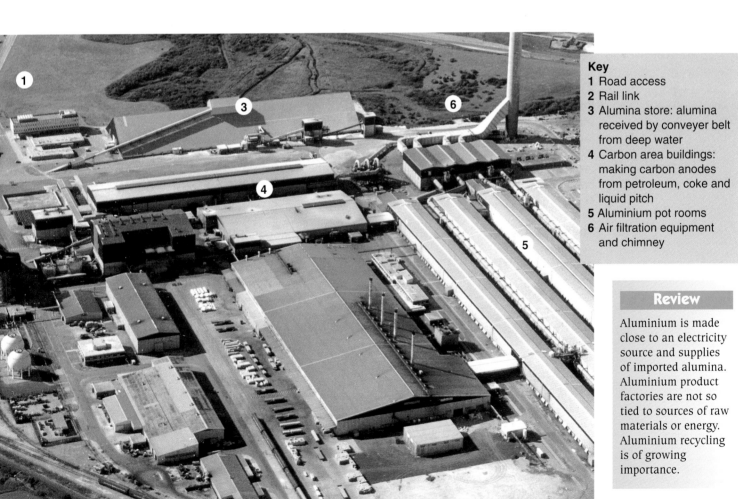

Key
1 Road access
2 Rail link
3 Alumina store: alumina received by conveyer belt from deep water
4 Carbon area buildings: making carbon anodes from petroleum, coke and liquid pitch
5 Aluminium pot rooms
6 Air filtration equipment and chimney

Review

Aluminium is made close to an electricity source and supplies of imported alumina. Aluminium product factories are not so tied to sources of raw materials or energy. Aluminium recycling is of growing importance.

CASE STUDY: The M4 Corridor and Swindon

Main activity

This exercise has data response questions and asks students to design a brochure for a new business park.

Key ideas

● To the west of London, a growth corridor has developed at the expense of London itself.
● Business parks and industrial estates have located near the M4 junctions.
● High-tech companies and Honda cars have found the region favourable.

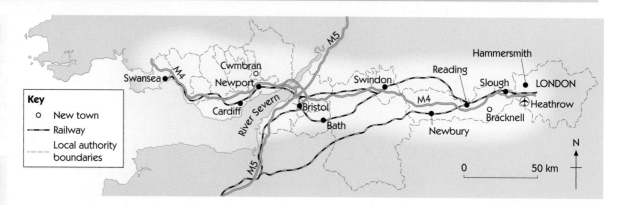

Figure A: Map of the M4 Corridor

This case study is about a **growth axis** that has developed to the west of London (Figure A). It has been called both the M4 Corridor and the Sunrise Strip. There are major differences in the physical geography of this economic region because it stretches from the London Basin through the upper Thames valley and the chalk and limestone of central southern England to the Severn Estuary in the west, and beyond into coastal South Wales. The population change along the corridor has varied too (Figure B). Figure C summarises the major reasons for the growth of this new economic region. The region's accessibility is perhaps the key to its success.

Swindon

Swindon has been a rapidly growing town since the 1950s when it became an overspill town for London. It was then a one industry railway town, and it wisely set about diversifying its employment. The present Rover factory, which makes body panels for the assembly factories in Oxford (Cowley), Birmingham (Longbridge) and

There has been a growth in high-tech industries and offices which are footloose (they do not have to be sited near a raw material). These industries did not have to grow in the older congested parts of the London region. They have taken advantage of:
● lower land costs and rent
● greenfield sites for factories
● less congested roads and services
● the M4 motorway and main line railway
● the proximity of Heathrow airport
● closeness to Channel ports and European markets
● nearness to universities and research establishments
● a large labour force some of whom have moved out of London into overspill towns
● lower house prices
● attractive environments
● local authorities wanting to attract employment

Figure C: Reasons for the growth of the M4 Corridor

Solihull, was opened in 1955. **High-tech** companies such as Plessey and Intel and EMI (making compact discs) have established in Swindon. It has also become a major office centre with the national headquarters of Allied Dunbar, Nationwide and Burmah Castrol. Woolworth, W. H. Smith and the Early Learning Centre have chosen Swindon for siting distribution warehouses.

On land once producing railway engines, Iceland Frozen Foods have built a distribution centre (Figure D). The site is close to Junction 16 of the M4. One of the main reasons for choosing Swindon was that the depot would have a large **sphere of influence**. Truck drivers are only allowed by law to drive for five hours before taking a rest, and a very large area of England and Wales can quickly be reached within five hours from Swindon.

Between the 1981 Census and the 1991 Census			
Counties	1981	1991	% change
Outer London	4,183,137	4,021,611	−4
Inner London	2,425,630	2,265,815	−7
Berkshire	675,000	716,500	+6
Wiltshire	518,000	553,300	+7
Avon	909,400	919,800	+1
Gwent	439,700	432,300	−2
S Glamorgan	384,700	383,300	−0.3
Mid Glamorgan	537,700	526,500	−2
W Glamorgan	367,300	357,800	−3

Figure B: Population change in the M4 Corridor region, London and South Wales

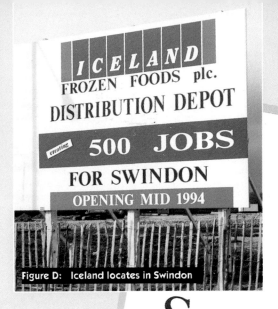

Figure D: Iceland locates in Swindon

ICELAND FROZEN FOODS plc.
DISTRIBUTION DEPOT
creating **500 JOBS**
FOR SWINDON
OPENING MID 1994

A VICKERS PROPERTIES DEVELOPMENT

South Marston PARK SWINDON

Successful location

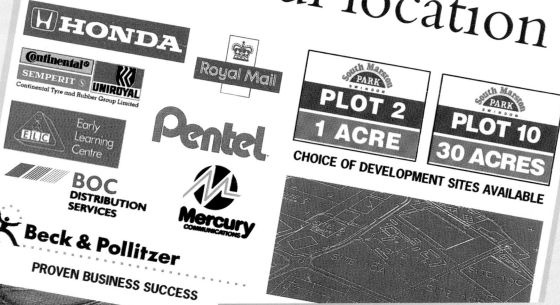

HONDA

Continental
SEMPERIT UNIROYAL
Continental Tyre and Rubber Group Limited

ELC Early Learning Centre

BOC DISTRIBUTION SERVICES

Beck & Pollitzer

PROVEN BUSINESS SUCCESS

Royal Mail

Pentel

Mercury COMMUNICATIONS

PLOT 2 1 ACRE   **PLOT 10 30 ACRES**

CHOICE OF DEVELOPMENT SITES AVAILABLE

250 ACRES IN MATURE PARKLAND

South Marston Park Swindon benefits from an exce... from the M4, giving easy access to London, Wales a... and points North and South. We can build to your sp... of mature parkland. And of course you'll be in good ...

Figure E: South Marston Park advertisement

▼ Questions

1. Describe the location of the M4 Corridor.
2. Why can the M4 Corridor be called an economic region?
3. Describe how the population changed along the M4 Corridor between 1981 and 1991.
4. Give reasons for the varied population changes along the Corridor.
5. a Draw a line graph to show the changes in Swindon's population from 1951 to 1991.

1951 90,570	*1961* 119,451	*1971* 139,355	*1981* 150,746	*1991* 170,850

   b When was Swindon's fastest period of growth?
   c What was the percentage increase in Swindon's population between 1981 and 1991? How did this compare with that of the whole county of Wiltshire (Figure B)?
6. How did Swindon diversify its employment?
7. Design an advertisement or brochure for a new business park in the M4 Corridor region. You can base some of your ideas on Figure E and the description of South Marston Park in the text.

Figure F: The Honda car plant in Swindon

The Honda car plant

Immediately to the south of the South Marston Park is the Honda European car assembly plant (Figure F). The new buildings are on the old South Marston airfield. Honda is a multi-national company with 76 production facilities in 36 countries. Their target is to make 150,000 Honda cars a year at Swindon with over 2000 employees. This represents 50% of European sales. If Japanese companies are to sell cars within the EU then 60% of the components they use must also be produced in the EU. This is why the company manufactures in Europe. As with other Japanese firms they favour location in the UK because of the English language and lower costs compared to some other EU countries.

Honda is the third Japanese car maker to base its European production in the UK. The first was Nissan, which chose an old airfield site between Sunderland and Washington in north east England. Toyota located near Derby and also chose an airfield site. Figure G shows Honda's six reasons for choosing to locate in Swindon. You should note that since establishing in Swindon, Honda and Rover have split up, and BMW has taken over the Rover division.

The total investment at Swindon is the considerable sum of £340 million. This will generate much more wealth for the local area. Swindon and the M4 Corridor region is now a part of Britain's core region attracting more and more development, a process known as the **multiplier effect** (see the Model of Growth page 55).

Do you know?

? Most leading car manufacturers have assembly plants in the UK.

? The car industry grew out of the coach building and bicycle industries.

? It was originally located in the West Midlands and South East England.

? The UK ranks about 7th in world production of motor cars.

? The map (Figure I) shows the distribution of the UK car industry.

Why did Honda come to Swindon?

History of Engineering in Swindon
● Ex-employees from the British Rail works provided a high quality workforce

Access to Rover Group
● Rover's body and pressing plant 3km away
● Rover Cowley 80km away
● Rover Longbridge 120km away

Good access to
● Ports at: Portsbury and Southampton
● Roads: M4, M25
● major rail links to Bristol and London
● Airport: Heathrow

Market
● Well situated for the total European Market

Large site
● 148 hectares (367 acres)
● Vickers Supermarine previously owned the site, their old runway is used for the test track

The Borough Council
● welcomed Honda
● no cash incentives
● wanted a mix of manufacturing and service industries

Figure G: Honda's reasons for locating in Swindon

Figure H: High-tech operations inside the Honda factory

Figure I: Car assembly and component plants in Britain

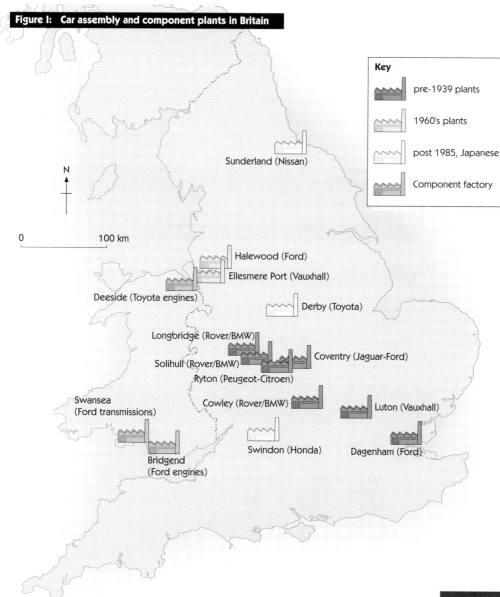

Key

- pre-1939 plants
- 1960's plants
- post 1985, Japanese
- Component factory

Sunderland (Nissan)

N

0 — 100 km

Halewood (Ford)
Ellesmere Port (Vauxhall)
Deeside (Toyota engines)
Derby (Toyota)
Longbridge (Rover/BMW)
Solihull (Rover/BMW)
Coventry (Jaguar-Ford)
Ryton (Peugeot-Citroen)
Swansea (Ford transmissions)
Cowley (Rover/BMW)
Luton (Vauxhall)
Swindon (Honda)
Dagenham (Ford)
Bridgend (Ford engines)

▼ Questions

8 What is meant by a **multi-national company**?

9 Why have Japanese car companies located production plants in Europe?

10 Why was the site at Swindon suitable for Honda?

11 Draw a diagram to show the location advantages of Swindon for the Honda factory.

12 How are the sites of the three Japanese car companies similar?

13 In a few sentences state why the Honda factory will generate more wealth for the Swindon area.

Review

The new economic developments in the M4 Corridor region are typical of the developed world's prosperous core regions. The reason why the area is so dynamic in its growth is because it is accessible to the UK and Europe.

CASE STUDY: South Wales – The Second Severn Crossing

Main activity

This activity includes response questions using the information provided. There are large scale maps and photographs to interpret.

Key ideas and questions

● This former coalfield and heavy industrial region has been revitalised.
● There have been government grants to help with infrastructure, industry and the environment.
● How has the region been revitalised?
● How has the Second Severn Crossing helped the region?
● What is the present role of the port of Swansea?
● How have the old docks been redeveloped?

In 1913 South Wales produced 56 million tonnes of coal with a workforce of 232,000. Much of the coal was used locally in metal manufacturing industries. There were iron and steel works, and tin, zinc, nickel and copper plants. In 1996 only 500,000 tonnes of coal were produced from one surviving colliery at Hirwaun, with a workforce of 239. There are now only two iron and steel works, one at Port Talbot and the other at Llanwern near Newport.

There has been financial help to revitalise the region's economy. The M4 motorway and the Head of the Valleys road have improved links with England. The iron and steel industry has been slimmed down and is now efficient and productive. Oil refining continues at Milford Haven and there are petrochemical works in the Swansea Bay area. Motor vehicle components are made in Swansea and Bridgend (Ford). There has been some **de-centralisation** of offices from London to South Wales. The DVLA (Driver and Vehicle Licensing Centre) is in Swansea, the Royal Mint in Llantrisant and the Inland Revenue and Ministry of Defence in Cardiff.

The Second Severn Crossing

Possibly the greatest impact of the new crossing will be in the boost it could give to investment opportunities in South Wales.
A consultancy report for the Welsh Development Agency.

Before the building of the Severn Bridge in 1966, South Wales was linked to England only through Gloucester, the lowest bridging point on the river Severn. This new network link helped to revitalise the declining mining and industrial region of South Wales. As road traffic in the M4 Corridor and South Wales increased, so the Severn Bridge became more and more congested. At times of repairs, high winds and accidents it could not bear the traffic. In 1996 the Second Severn Crossing was opened making Bristol 14 kilometres nearer Cardiff (see Figure A) by road. Figure B has some viewpoints about the new crossing which were reported in local Bristol and Welsh newspapers. The newspaper article (Figure C) gives details about possible developments on the Welsh side of the bridge.

Advantages	Disadvantages
● There should be less holiday hold-ups	● The new M49 link cuts across land planned for a sports stadium
● There will be improved links for business in South Wales	● New industrial estates will destroy rural land
● The new bridge will be 'wind shielded' to protect traffic	● Greenbelt land may become threatened
● Magor in Wales may become a dormitory town for the Bristol area	● With more growth the area could suffer even more traffic problems
● New industries and offices will be attracted to the region	● More concrete and tarmac mean more flood risk as 'run-off' increases

Figure B: Viewpoints about the second Severn crossing

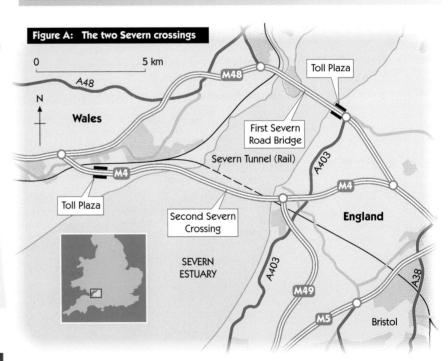

Figure A: The two Severn crossings

The new crossing has already been of benefit to the Cardiff/Newport/Chepstow axis. The South Korean company LG is building factories for semiconductors and consumer electronics at Imperial Park in Newport. Over 6000 jobs will be created. This is Europe's largest **inward investment** and should act as a magnet for more foreign investment. Newport is a government Intermediate Area for funding (Figure D). The LC development has been funded at the equivalent of about £30,000 per job, which some people say is too much.

Tesco has built a warehouse and distribution centre at Gwent Europark near Magor. The distribution group Christian Salvesen has a new warehouse at Chepstow. Land here is cheap and there is plenty available, and this will encourage more investment.

Short drive to extra commuter belt: Welsh Boon

On the Welsh side of the second Severn Bridge lie three villages whose names are little known to most people on the other side of the estuary.

But once the new bridge is open Magor, Undy and Rogiet will become as familiar as Chepstow.

Magor is currently a picturesque village only half-an-hour's drive from Cardiff and Bristol. But the opening of the new bridge will see the community and its surrounding hamlets bear the brunt of what is sure to become Wales' new "golden corridor".

From the existing Magor interchange on the M4 the new approach road to the bridge will be four miles long. And between the Magor Interchange and a new one at Undy, the existing M4 will be widened to provide and extra lane in each direction.

The new approach will cross the B4245 and the railway to approach the estuary over Caldicot Moor, passing south of Rogiet and Caldicot.

The construction of the bridge runs in tandem with Gwent borough council's plan to redevelop the area over the next 15 years. It is envisaged a regional airport will be built near Redwick, just a mile away from Magor.

Land south of the motorway is earmarked for housing, and property prices will probably be cheaper than in Bristol.

With the main rail line into Wales running just south of Magor, the village will become a dormitory town for Bristol, Newport and Cardiff, and home to thousands of commuters.

Magor can expect to follow Chepstow's experience after the first Severn Bridge came to its door.

'Once it was home to people from the valleys, men who moved from Ebbw Vale to work at the Llanwern Steel Works,' says Mr Andrew Griffith, managing director of Herbert Lewis, the town's biggest department store.

'Today we're more popular with managers and middle-managers and company executives.'

'The population has grown by almost 30 per cent in the last 20 years. And house prices are much higher.'

Adapted from *Welsh Daily Press*, 18 August 1992

Figure C: What will happen on the Welsh side after the new crossing?

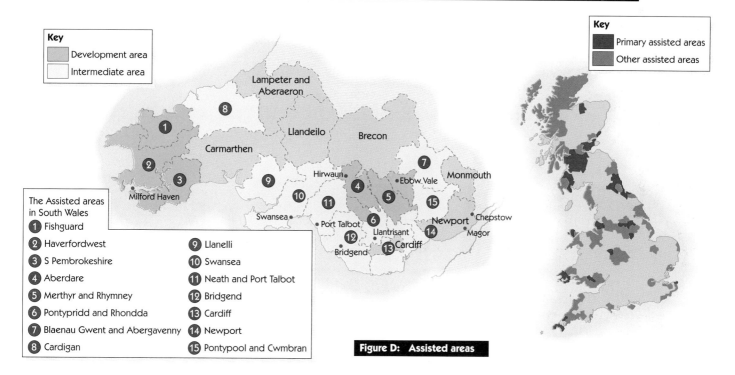

Key
- Development area
- Intermediate area

The Assisted areas in South Wales
1. Fishguard
2. Haverfordwest
3. S Pembrokeshire
4. Aberdare
5. Merthyr and Rhymney
6. Pontypridd and Rhondda
7. Blaenau Gwent and Abergavenny
8. Cardigan
9. Llanelli
10. Swansea
11. Neath and Port Talbot
12. Bridgend
13. Cardiff
14. Newport
15. Pontypool and Cwmbran

Key
- Primary assisted areas
- Other assisted areas

Figure D: Assisted areas

▼ Questions

1. Where is the Second Severn Crossing?
2. Why was it built?
3. Choose two advantages and two disadvantages from the viewpoints in Figure B. Explain the reasoning behind the viewpoints.
4. Study the newspaper article (Figure C).
   a. Which villages may become dormitory towns?
   b. To where will commuters travel?
   c. How will house prices compare to Bristol?
   d. Why will Magor be like Chepstow?
   e. Who once moved into the Magor area from Ebbw Vale?
   f. What do you think might eventually happen to traffic flows, land availability, and house prices in the Magor areas?
5. 'Economic prosperity follows lines of communication.' To what extent will the Second Severn Crossing encourage more prosperity to the east of South Wales? ➡
6. Why do you think some people believe that too much money is being given to LG for their new factory development?

The port of Swansea

The port of Swansea has well established trade with northern Europe, the Mediterranean and Ireland. Its main features can be seen on Figure E. Its trade is diverse and is linked to local oil, petrochemical, metal and construction industries. In the past the port specialised in coal and metal exports and the import of raw materials for the local heavy industries. The port handles tinplate, steel, aluminium, coal, timber, cement and sand.

The old docks now form part of the Swansea Maritime Quarter. In 1975 this area was identified as an area for regeneration. There was investment in housing and businesses, in the development of the water area and in the re-development of derelict land. Figure E shows some of the present developments in this area. Funding for regeneration has come from public and private sources. There have been grants from the Welsh Development Agency and the European Regional Fund for Development as well as loans from the European Investment Bank. It is an Intermediate Area for government assistance (Figure D on page 63).

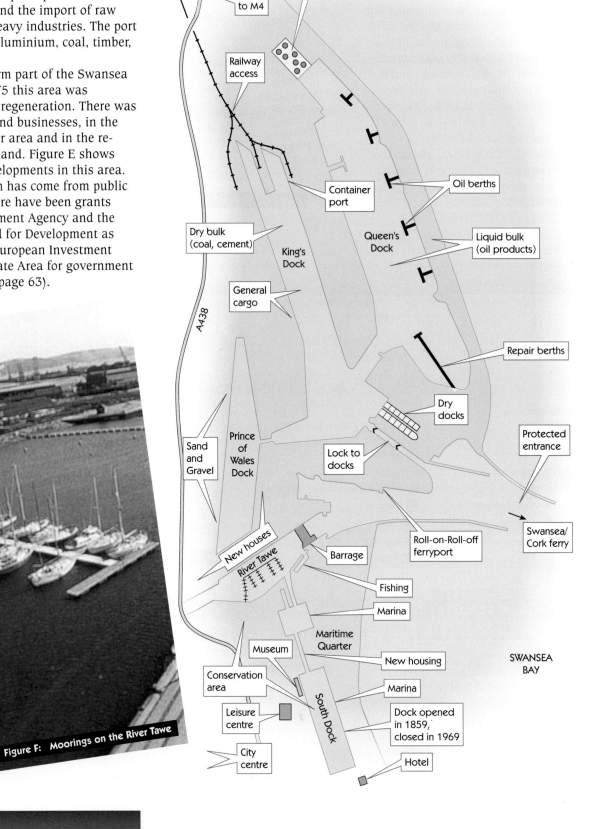

Figure E: The present port of Swansea and new developments

0   500 km

Oil storage (tank farms)

Link to M4

Railway access

Container port

Oil berths

Dry bulk (coal, cement)

King's Dock

Queen's Dock

Liquid bulk (oil products)

General cargo

Repair berths

A438

Dry docks

Sand and Gravel

Prince of Wales Dock

Lock to docks

Protected entrance

Swansea/ Cork ferry

New houses

River Tawe

Barrage

Roll-on-Roll-off ferryport

Fishing

Marina

Maritime Quarter

Museum

New housing

SWANSEA BAY

Conservation area

South Dock

Marina

Leisure centre

Dock opened in 1859, closed in 1969

City centre

Hotel

Figure F: Moorings on the River Tawe

The Swansea Bay Barrage has been important in improving the River Tawe. It was built to retain water within the tidal reaches. There is a small hydro-generator built into the barrage which produces enough electricity to power 300 street lights. There is a fish pass which allows spawning salmon to pass up-river. A family of grey seals has also moved in! The barrage provided the incentive for the marinas to be built; it cleaned up the waterfront and led to improvement of the river banks. The river now appears clean and is the focal point for the new developments. Today there are over 600 marina berths, over 1000 new homes, an industrial maritime museum, a theatre, restaurant and leisure centre. In the **conservation area** houses built in the early 1800s have been refurbished as flats.

Up-river from the barrage is the site of Britain's first and largest Enterprise Zone which was in existence from 1981 to 1994. Over 6000 jobs were created in the zone (Figure G). A large area of derelict land was re-developed and the present Swansea Enterprise Park ranks as one of the best business parks in Britain. Today the Swansea Bay Partnership oversees developments in the Park.

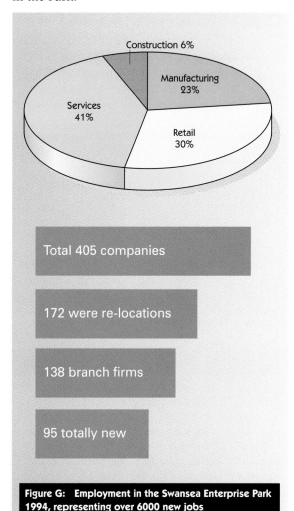

Figure G: Employment in the Swansea Enterprise Park 1994, representing over 6000 new jobs

Do you know?

? **Roll-on-Roll-off (Ro-Ro)** ships carrying road freight vehicles

? **Container** a standard sized unit carried by rail, road and ship

? **Bulk cargoes** goods such as coal and cement (dry) and oil (liquid)

? **Tidal harbour** a harbour where the water moves up and down (in and out) with the tides

? **Docks** protected water which remains at the same level, controlled by locks

? **Enterprise zone** a small zone designated for urban renewal with financial incentives

? **Re-development, revitalisation, regeneration, renewal** all words describing areas which are being modernised and rebuilt

? **Refurbishing** refers to buildings which are being modernised without being rebuilt

▼ Questions

1 Study the map of the port of Swansea (Figure E).
  a Match the following port activities with correct location on the map.

Port Activity	Location
General cargo handling	Dry docks
Off-loading oil	Marina
Handling sand and gravel	Queen's Dock
Inspecting damage to ships	Container Port
Leisure boating	King's Dock
Unloading containers	Ferryport
Travelling to Ireland	Prince of Wales Dock

  b Outline the re-developments to the west of the main port.
2 a How has the barrage changed the surrounding river environment?
  b In what ways can the building of a barrage upset the coastal environment? ➡
3 a State the purpose of the Swansea Enterprise Zone.
  b How has the Enterprise Zone affected local employment?
4 Extension question
    Discuss the recent changes that have taken place in a coastal port that you have studied. ➡

Do you know?

? As ports have been modernised throughout the UK the old docks have been abandoned. Dockland re-development is an important part of inner-city revitalisation.

? Cardiff: new barrage and developments in Cardiff Bay

? London: the largest development of old docks at Docklands (see page 76)

? Salford: new dockland development in Manchester

? Also Hull, Liverpool and Bristol

South Wales: Clydach Vale

Development: costs and benefits

There has been considerable financial help from various agencies to redevelop South Wales. The benefits are usually clear to see, to read about and experience. The costs, however, are not always reckoned. Figure H lists some of them.

Economic

Swansea attracts more money for the Enterprise Zone	*jobs are drawn in from nearby areas not attracting money* *job displacement*
LG move to Newport	*another area did not get the investment*
People move to Magor to be a part of the new development axis	*another area will continue to lose people and house prices there will drop*

Social

Young and dynamic people move home	*the older and poorer people will be left in the old settlements*
New housing areas such as in the Swansea Maritime Quarter do not attract families	*they are not socially balanced*

Environmental

The approach road for the Second Severn Crossing crosses the Gwent Levels	*it might upset water quality and wildlife*
New development around the new bridge is mainly attracted to flat arable land	*it is then lost*
New barrages are built *(The Cardiff Bay Barrage is a larger scheme than the Swansea barrage)*	*tidal flows are disturbed mudflats essential for wading birds are destroyed.*

Figure H: The costs of development

Clydach Vale

Clydach Vale is an old coal mining settlement in a tributary valley of the Rhondda Fawr. It can be found on the Ordnance Survey 1:50,000 map Sheet 170 at grid reference 9792/9892. Figure I is an extract from a larger scale map, the 1:10,560 (6 inches=1 mile) map dated 1965. The grid squares are the same as those on the 1:50,000 map at 1 kilometre apart. The photograph (Figure J) was taken 30 years after the map was published. The transformation from a derelict mining landscape to the modern Cambrian Business Park is typical of changes in many South Wales mining valleys.

▼ Questions

1 In what ways does the old 1:10,560 map differ from the 1:50,000 maps?

2 Describe the buildings and the landscapes shown on the map.

3 Link up the map with the photograph. In which direction was the camera pointing?

4 Either:
  a Describe the changes shown on the photograph compared with the map, or
  b Draw a labelled sketch of the photograph to show the present buildings and landscape, and in a different colour label what used to be there.

5 a Suggest the type of activities which may take place at the Cambrian Business Park.
  b How has the government helped new industry to locate in an area like Clydach Vale?
  c What do you think are the costs and benefits of the Cambrian Business Park development? ➧

6 You are an older male worker at one of the new factories. Compare life now with that when the Welsh valleys were coal mining areas. ➧

Review

The revitalisation of the South Wales region has been helped by government grants and effective planning processes. The Second Severn Crossing will help to consolidate South Wales as a modern manufacturing region. Swansea has been helped by the developments in the Enterprise Zone and the re-development of the old docks. Large scale maps can be used to analyse the geography of a small area.

Figure I: Extract from 1:10,560 map of Clydach Vale

Figure J: Cambrian Business Park

4

The population of south west England

Main activity

This activity is based on interpreting population maps.

Key ideas and questions

● Population distribution is uneven and is influenced by physical and human factors.
● Population change is the combined result of natural change and migration.
● South west England is a fast growing region.
● Why does the south west attract migrants?
● Which other regions also attract migrants and which regions have high out-migration rates?

The two maps (Figures A and B) have been drawn as **choropleth** or **density shading** maps using the results of the 1991 census. Every ten years in the UK there is a census. Every household receives a questionnaire about the number of people in the household, their age, employment and other details (see the Birmingham census details on page 79). It is by comparing information from censuses that changes can be seen.

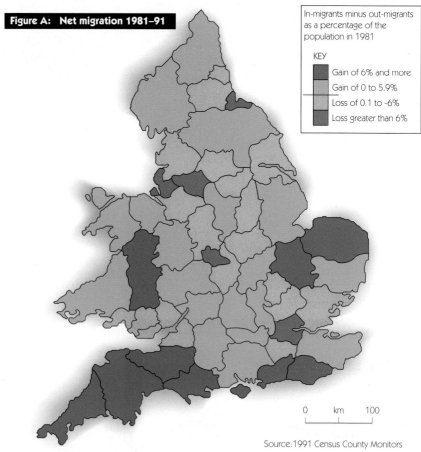

Figure A: Net migration 1981–91

In-migrants minus out-migrants as a percentage of the population in 1981

KEY
Gain of 6% and more
Gain of 0 to 5.9%
Loss of 0.1 to -6%
Loss greater than 6%

0   km   100

Source:1991 Census County Monitors

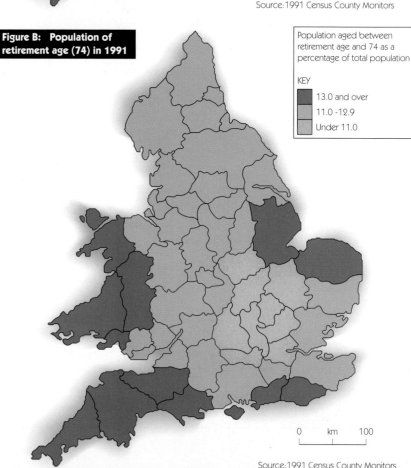

Figure B: Population of retirement age (74) in 1991

Population aged between retirement age and 74 as a percentage of total population

KEY
13.0 and over
11.0 -12.9
Under 11.0

0   km   100

Source:1991 Census County Monitors

▼ Questions

1 For each of the maps, Figures A and B, describe the pattern of population distribution. You should name a few of the counties with highest and the lowest figures on each map.
2 Suggest reasons for the pattern of net migration on Figure A.
3 Give reasons for the differences between Figures A and B.

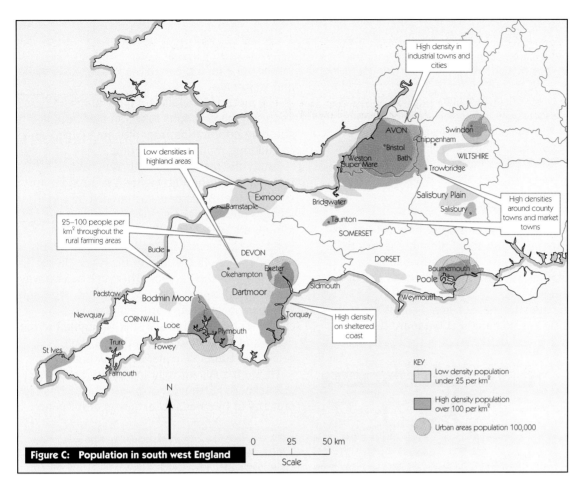

Figure C: Population in south west England

KEY

- Low density population under 25 per km²
- High density population over 100 per km²
- Urban areas population 100,000

High density in industrial towns and cities

Low densities in highland areas

25–100 people per km² throughout the rural farming areas

High densities around county towns and market towns

High density on sheltered coast

0   25   50 km
Scale

N

Labels on map: AVON, Swindon, Chippenham, Bristol, Bath, WILTSHIRE, Weston Super Mare, Trowbridge, Exmoor, Bridgwater, Salisbury Plain, Salisbury, Barnstaple, Taunton, SOMERSET, Bude, DEVON, DORSET, Bournemouth, Okehampton, Exeter, Poole, Sidmouth, Weymouth, Padstow, Bodmin Moor, Dartmoor, Torquay, Newquay, CORNWALL, Looe, Plymouth, St Ives, Truro, Fowey, Falmouth

---

South West England and the census

The map of south west England (Figure C) shows the distribution of population and the labels give reasons for the distribution. Figure D shows some of the recent changes in population. The south west economic planning region shown in Figures C and D grew by 5.5% between 1981 and 1991. The fastest growing region in the country was East Anglia with 7.7% growth.

▼ Questions

4 Use Figure C to describe the population distribution in the south west region.

5 Explain the distribution of population in the south west.

6 Use Figure D to describe and explain the population changes in the south west. ➤

7 Why do you think that the south west is particularly attractive to people of retirement age?

Review

Census statistics can be used to analyse a whole range of population characteristics at a range of scales. The south west is a fast growing region attracting in-migration.

Figure D: Population changes in the south west

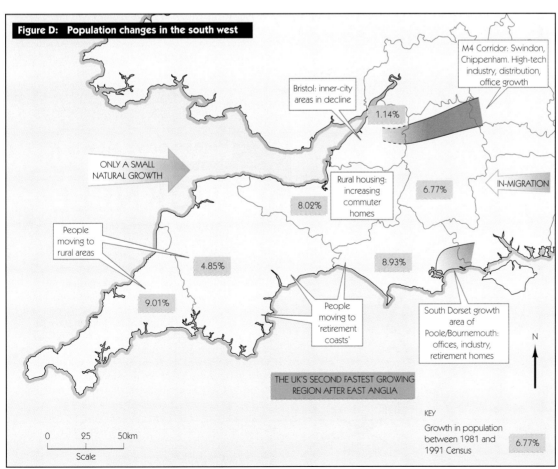

ONLY A SMALL NATURAL GROWTH

Bristol: inner-city areas in decline

M4 Corridor: Swindon, Chippenham. High-tech industry, distribution, office growth

1.14%

Rural housing: increasing commuter homes

6.77%

IN-MIGRATION

8.02%

People moving to rural areas

4.85%

8.93%

9.01%

People moving to 'retirement coasts'

South Dorset growth area of Poole/Bournemouth: offices, industry, retirement homes

THE UK'S SECOND FASTEST GROWING REGION AFTER EAST ANGLIA

N

0   25   50km
Scale

KEY

Growth in population between 1981 and 1991 Census

6.77%

Key ideas and question

- Bicester has a small rural sphere of influence.
- Its market town functions have changed and growth has brought problems.
- Has sensitive planning maintained the small town atmosphere of Bicester despite its rapid growth?

Main activity

This is written as an enquiry to which students can respond, and to follow in their own enquiry work. Questions are based on a road map, photographs and the issues of planning for growth and conservation.

The Bicester Enquiry

The **aim** is to answer a range of questions on Bicester and be aware of planning issues that affect small towns. You should also be in a position to use the enquiry methods to carry out similar surveys.

The **questions** are: Where is it? What is it like? How is it changing? What are the strengths and weaknesses of the town? What can be done to improve the town for local people and visitors?

The **methods** include studying maps, analysing photographs taken on fieldwork, studying information from planning papers and considering proposals for action.

Study the **results** of the surveys and information gathering. Figure A is a road map showing that Bicester is surrounded by small villages and is linked to the M40 motorway joining the West Midlands with Oxford and London. The land is flat and drained by small streams which flow south to the River Cherwell, a tributary of the Thames. There are two railway lines, one linking Bicester with Oxford, although the line shown to the north east has been closed. The other link is with Birmingham to the north and London to the south east (fast commuter trains take just over one hour).

Figure B gives information about the village of Bucknell (north west of Bicester) which is one of many in Bicester's rural sphere of influence.

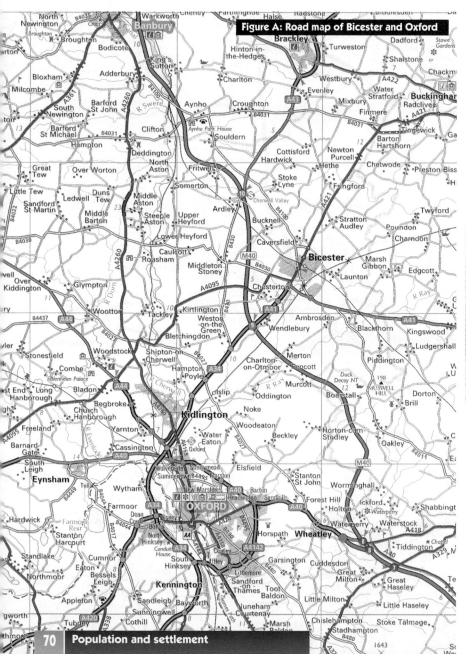

Figure A: Road map of Bicester and Oxford

The village is sited on a small ridge of higher land at 100 metres above sea level; a small stream flows south east from the village. The small and **nucleated** settlement has developed at a crossroads. The village dates back many centuries; it has a Manor House and a Manor Farm. Bucknell is at the bottom of the hierarchy with some isolated farms around the village. It is surrounded by low lying land between 90 and 100 metres above sea level. The land use is a mix of crops and pasture.

The M40 Junction 10 is just to the north of the village. The village has a small post office combined with a village store. There is a pub with a garden and a church. There are no schools and children have to travel to Bicester. The community has a village hall and a new recreation ground was opened in 1997. So far there is no large scale **impact** of the M40 link in terms of building. There are five new houses in the village and some farm barns have been converted for offices and studios. The noise from the M40 is however intrusive and there has been an increase in through traffic since the motorway was built.

Figure B: The village of Bucknell

Bicester is a part of the Cherwell District of Oxfordshire. The graph (Figure C) shows the population growth for the district compared to the city of Oxford. Bicester is the fastest growing town in Oxfordshire and has a population of over 22,000. The planning map (Figure D) outlines some of the main features of Bicester's recent and future development. There are fewer jobs in Bicester than the number of working people. A factory shopping outlet called Bicester Village has been built to the south of the town. It is isolated from the main town by a playing field area. It advertises itself as a retail development near to the M40; it does not link itself closely to Bicester town centre. The village has provided a number of low paid service jobs but more employment is needed for Bicester if commuting is to be limited.

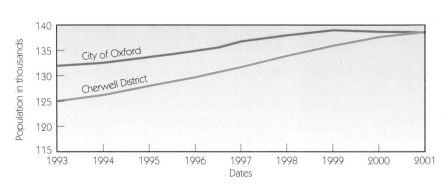

Figure C: The growing Cherwell District

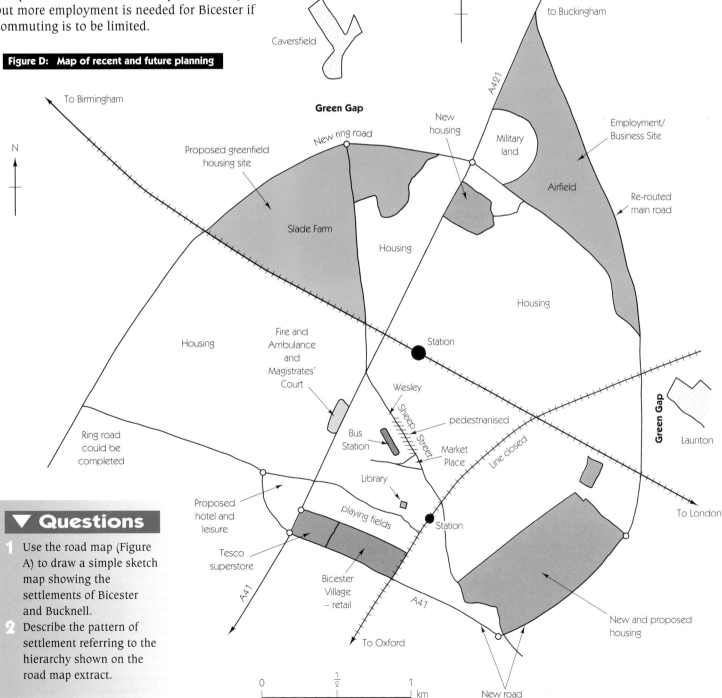

Figure D: Map of recent and future planning

▼ Questions

1 Use the road map (Figure A) to draw a simple sketch map showing the settlements of Bicester and Bucknell.

2 Describe the pattern of settlement referring to the hierarchy shown on the road map extract.

Key elements in
Figure E

● cleaned up shop fronts
● traditional lampposts
● raised planted beds
  with trees
● flower tubs
● traditional clock tower
● bollards to exclude
  vehicles
● litter bin
● safe and smooth paved
  pedestrian street

Issues arising from the planning proposals

● Should the Slade Farm **greenfield site** be developed for 2000 houses.
● Is the development of the airfield for business use a good idea?
● Should the A421 road be re-routed around Bicester and the ring road completed?
● Should 'green' gaps be preserved between the town and the villages?
● Should housing expansion in the south west only be allowed if the Bicester/Oxford rail link is improved?

Figure G is a summary of the Bicester Urban Design Strategy. This planning strategy was produced by Cherwell District Council because:
● development is being pushed its way i.e. away from Oxford
● Bicester is likely to grow anyway because of the M40 and relatively cheap house prices
● there has not really been any similar planning strategy before.

Strengths
● Good access to surrounding towns and to London and Birmingham
● Strong centre for local people
● Character of a market town with historic core remains
● Good local variety of shops
● Housing relatively cheap
● Bicester Village is drawing people in

Weaknesses
● Internal traffic problems
● People visiting Bicester Village do not visit Bicester itself
● Empty buildings
● Lacks an identifiable centre
● The centre is dead in the evenings
● Lack of restaurants and eating places

Opportunities
● Shopping centre can be developed
● Bicester Village should have more benefits for the town
● A ring road would reduce congestion in the town
● Re-routing of the A421 would take traffic out of Bicester

Threats
● Bicester could grow too fast in the future
● The traditional character could be lost
● The town could suffer further traffic congestion

Figure E: Pedestrianised Sheep Street

Key elements in
Figure F

● clearly labelled
  pedestrian zone
● disabled vehicle access
  only
● no cycling
● street bench
● raised planted beds
  faced in local stone
● large area of traffic-free
  street

The town centre

The older part of Bicester has a medieval street pattern and there is a conservation area centred on the Market Place. The old shopping street has been pedestrianised and made 'user-friendly' (Figures E and F). The small Wesley Row arcade has preserved some old small town atmosphere (Figure I).

Figure F: Traffic prohibited in Sheep Street

Why not more pedestrianisation?

We have no real focus for the town

Strengths   Weaknesses

Opportunities   Threats

Why not more restaurants?

We work to cut down on through traffic

Figure G: The Urban Design Strategy

Figure I: The Wesley Road Arcade, preserving the old character of the town

To reach its conclusions Cherwell District Council analysed the strengths, weaknesses, opportunities and threats: a SWOT analysis. The Town Action Plan is summarised in Figure H.

The **analysis** and **conclusion** of this enquiry will be completed by you answering the questions.

Change the form of the town by pedestrianising Market Square

Improve life and vitality
- Preserve the centre as a market town
- Improve street furniture
- Encourage small shops and cafes
- Provide a central multi-purpose building with cinema and theatre

Improve economic viability
- Invest in Market Square
- Improve links with Bicester Village
- Provide signs to 'Historic Bicester' from the M40

Improve accessibility
- Provide disability access
- Improve cycleways
- Provide a public transport link to Bicester village
- Provide out-of-town parking

Improve safety
- Renew the street lighting
- Encourage people to live in the centre
- Encourage housing above shops
- Develop more facilities to give life in the evenings

Figure H: Some features of the Action Plan

▼ Questions

3 Study the planning map (Figure D).
- a Which issue is linked to housing growth? What would be the impact of new housing on Bicester?
- b Which issue is linked to increasing employment? Why does the town need more employment?
- c Which improvements could be made to reduce traffic congestion?
- d In what ways could the countryside around Bicester be preserved?

3 Study the photographs of the town centre. How has the main shopping street been made more 'user-friendly'?

4 What is a SWOT analysis? What do you think are the two most important findings of the analysis in terms of:
- a strengths and
- b weaknesses?

5 In what ways do you think the town has opportunities to improve?

6 Draw a spray diagram to show the Action Plan for the town. Add to the diagram your own examples of how it can be improved for the future.

7 In conclusion, write about Bicester in the future. Use the following headings: The Town Centre, A Town for Living in, A Town for Working in, Traffic in and around Bicester.

Review

Bicester is typical of small towns. It needs to provide new housing, improve its shopping and increase its employment. This has to be done alongside managing traffic and conserving the old character of the town and the countryside around.

CASE STUDY: London – changing the inner city

Main activity

In this exercise the main activity is analysing changes and summarising new developments in Docklands.

Key ideas

● Port functions and industries have changed location.
● Congestion and high costs in the city have led to decentralisation, including moving to Docklands.
● People have moved away from the inner city.
● Inner city problems have been tackled in various ways.

Link up the photograph (Figure A) with the map of part of the London Docklands (Figure B). This is an area of the borough of Newham in east London where the old docks closed in 1981. The area then showed all the symptoms of inner-city decay. The port functions had moved, some downstream to modern roll-on-roll-off and container facilities at Tilbury. Manufacturing industry accounted for 33% of Docklands employment in 1981. This was declining rapidly as companies moved away to new locations or closed down as there was no longer demand for their products. The population of the area was declining with an average decline of minus 14.9% between 1971 and 1981. This was a faster decline than inner London as a whole (at minus 7.6%).

Such inner city decline and decay was not unique to London in 1981. Other major conurbations had similar problem areas. In the case of London there was also the problem of

Do you know?

? **Inner city**, the old residential and industrial area includes the **transitional zone**
? **LDDC**, London Docklands Development Corporation set up to regenerate the area in 1981 and ceasing in different areas 1994–98
? **Enterprise Zone**, established for the Isle of Dogs 1982–92
? **New Towns**, built with government money 8 built in a ring around London, later Milton Keynes a New City
? **Expanded Towns** towns receiving London **overspill** population resulting from the house-building agreements with local authorities

congestion in the areas surrounding Docklands including the nearby City where over 250,000 people worked. Since 1940 people had been moving out of London, a process called counter-urbanisation. Many of those who moved out to the Expanded Towns, the New Towns or surrounding rural areas still travelled to work in the centre. The population of Greater London had fallen from 8.6 million in 1939 to 6.71 million in 1981.

Changes in Docklands since 1981

Figure C summarises the main achievements of the Docklands re-development and some of the issues that remain. The mix of private and public investment and a strong vision from the Development Corporation has changed the image of Docklands. House building companies use the new positive image in their advertisements (Figure D on page 76). The development continues with the University of East London's new campus (1999). It is funded by major east London companies such as Ford and Tate and Lyle, as well as by the government's Single Regeneration Budget.

Docklands redevelopment

● Planning and finance	LDDC and Enterprise Zone
● The image	redrawn with marketing and advertising – now a positive place
● New offices	low rents compared with the City
● Employment	1981: 27,213 1996: 69,975
● Housing	over 20,000 new homes
● Home ownership	1981: 5% 1996: 40%
● Tourism	a tourist plan drawn up. 1.6 million visitors in 1995
● Population	1981: 39,429 1996: 76,849 2006 (est.): 106,715
● Infrastructure	London City Airport, Docklands Light Railway (DLR), Jubilee Line extension, new roads
● Local resistance	the development does not always benefit the local people: there is not enough cheap housing
● The property slump	between 1989 and 1992 some Docklands companies were declared bankrupt, and it could happen again
● Employment	is often for people commuting in and not for local people
● Community	the old sense of a Docklands community has been lost

Figure C: Docklands re-development

Figure A: View looking west across the old area of the Royal Docks towards Canary Wharf and central London

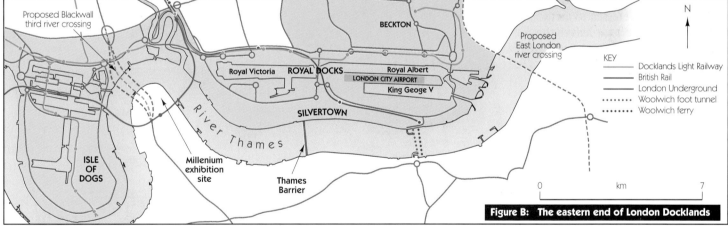

Figure B: The eastern end of London Docklands

▼ Questions

1 Study Figures A and B, the photograph and map of the Royal Docks.

a What is the name of the long dock in the centre of the photograph?

b Name three types of modern transport shown on the photograph.

c Describe the land use to the north of the docks.

d Why do you think the University of East London chose this as the site of their new campus?

e Using the photograph, where can local people work in the area immediately around these former docks?

2 What types of inner city decay would there have been in this area of docklands before 1981? ⬅

3 a List the different developments and achievements in this area since 1981.

b Why has it been so important to build up the transport infrastructure?

4 What do you think was the basis for local complaints about the re-development of these docklands in terms of employment and housing? ⬅

London – changing land and population

Changing industrial land in London

Inner city industrial areas are being redeveloped in parts of London as well as Docklands. Battersea Power Station south of Victoria railway station on the south bank of the Thames operated for 42 years before it closed in 1972. It is being developed as a cinema complex. Alongside will be hotels, theatres and exhibition space. Further upstream on the north bank of the river is another inner city industrial site at Chelsea. The old gas works here at Imperial Wharf had to be decontaminated and was then re-developed with housing, industry and leisure facilities. The Greenwich peninsula site for the Millennium exhibition is another example of former industrial land which had to be cleaned up and serviced with a new infrastructure before development could take place (see Figure B on page 75).

Population changes

Between the 1981 census and that of 1991 there was a decrease of 4.9% in the population of Greater London and a decrease of 6.6% in Inner London. The loss of people from the central areas of cities has been referred to as the 'doughnut effect' as it leaves the centre with a 'hole'. In the case of London, people have been encouraged back to live in the Docklands area. There is one borough, Tower Hamlets, with a population increase. Here there are higher birth rates, low outward migration, and people are moving into the borough. Children under 16 years old made up 19.5% of Greater London but in Tower Hamlets the figure was highest at 25.6%.

The map of population change, combining natural and migration change, (Figure E) shows the contrast between inner and outer London. Figure F shows the changes of the population in inner and outer London since 1891.

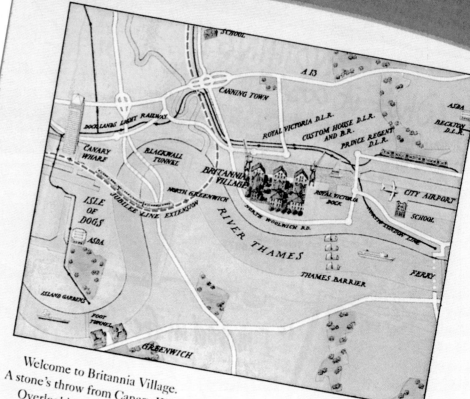

Figure D: Advertisement for Wimpey Homes

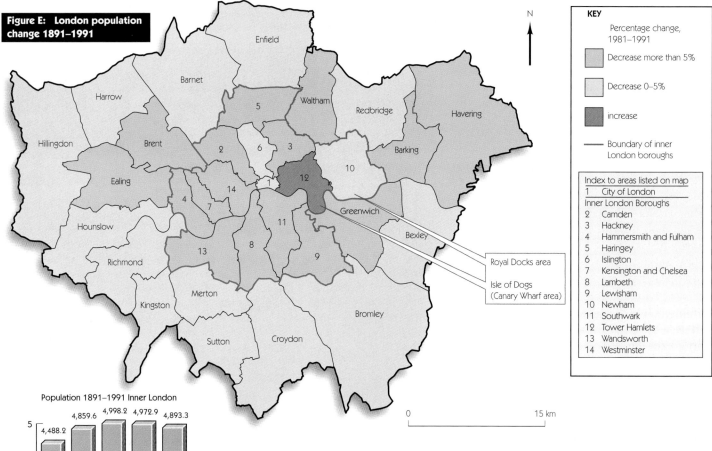

Figure E: London population change 1891–1991

KEY

Percentage change, 1981–1991

- Decrease more than 5%
- Decrease 0–5%
- increase

— Boundary of inner London boroughs

Index to areas listed on map
1   City of London

Inner London Boroughs
2   Camden
3   Hackney
4   Hammersmith and Fulham
5   Haringey
6   Islington
7   Kensington and Chelsea
8   Lambeth
9   Lewisham
10 Newham
11 Southwark
12 Tower Hamlets
13 Wandsworth
14 Westminster

Royal Docks area

Isle of Dogs (Canary Wharf area)

0   15 km

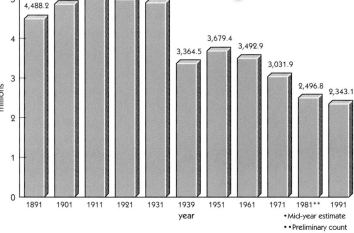

Population 1891–1991 Inner London

- Mid-year estimate
- Preliminary count

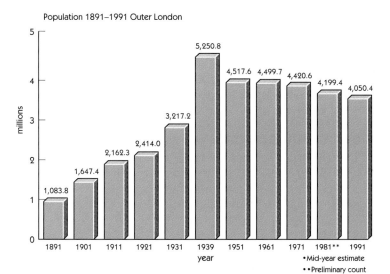

Population 1891–1991 Outer London

- Mid-year estimate
- Preliminary count

Figure F: Graphs to show population change in London 1891–1991

▼ Questions

5 Study the advertisement for the new homes (Figure D). Design your own advertisement for the new East London University to be sited to the north of the Royal Docks.

6 Study Figures E and F. Describe the changes in London's population:
a   between 1981 and 1991
b   since 1891 ➡

7 Account for the changes in terms of **push and pull factors**. ➡

8 Account for the recent increase in the population of Tower Hamlets.

9 Suggest what the 2001 census will reveal about the Borough of Newham.

Review

A variety of developments have changed the geography of the Royal Docks area of Docklands. The history of planning and development processes operating in this area are similar to those elsewhere in inner city areas.

CASE STUDY: Birmingham – living in a metropolis

Main activity

The main activities in this exercise are analysing and interpreting census statistics, maps, photographs and a planning application.

Key ideas

● Birmingham has a wide variety of living environments with wide cultural diversity.
● The inner areas are being re-developed for the twenty-first century.
● The area near the NEC and airport is an example of planned development.

Birmingham is the centre of the West Midlands and used to be known as the 'workshop of the world' and 'the city of a thousand trades'. In 1931, 37% of all employment in industry was in metal trades. More recently Birmingham became very dependent on the motor car and lost its broad range of manufacturing industries. The Birmingham area still has a high **Location Quotient** for manufacturing industry and a low Location Quotient for financial and business services. The region has above national average unemployment rates, a high population density, and a high percentage of people from non-white ethnic groups. The 1991 ethnic breakdown is shown in Figure A.

This project will extend the succeessful processes of regeneration to the west of the CBD and to the east of the centre around Digbeth
    Funded by a £50 million grant from the Lottery (Millenium Commission), the EU, local councils and private companies
    Creating over 1600 jobs
    Encouraging around half a million visitors a year to a Discovery Centre and the Hub which will be the social centre of the development
    Establishing a Technology Innovation Centre to help small firms
    Providing a learning experiences for young people at the University of the First Age
    Improving the environment and the canal network
    (Other Millenium Commission Landmark Projects include The Millenium Stadium in Cardiff, Hampden: Scotland's Field of Dreams in Glasgow and the Earth Centre in Doncaster)

Figure C: Millenium Point

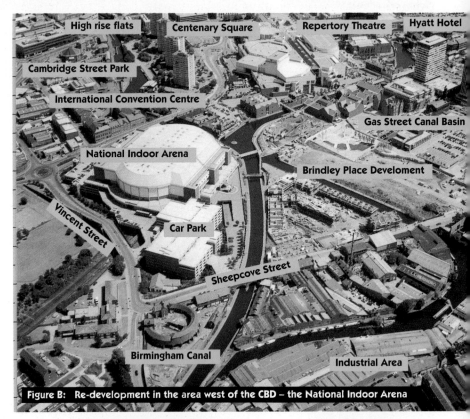

High rise flats   Centenary Square   Repertory Theatre   Hyatt Hotel
Cambridge Street Park
International Convention Centre
Gas Street Canal Basin
National Indoor Arena
Brindley Place Develoment
Vincent Street
Car Park
Sheepcove Street
Birmingham Canal
Industrial Area

Figure B: Re-development in the area west of the CBD – the National Indoor Arena

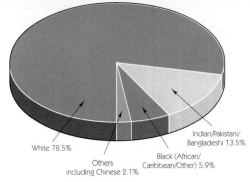

White 78.5%
Others including Chinese 2.1%
Black (African/ Caribbean/Other) 5.9%
Indian/Pakistani/ Bangladeshi 13.5%

Figure A: Birmingham residents by ethnic group

The total population of the Birmingham census district (shown on Figures D and E) fell by 3.5% between 1991 and 1981. This is typical of other large cities in Britain. The inner areas of the city declined the most, e.g. Nechells down 11.6%, whereas some of the outer wards increased, e.g. Sutton New Hall up by 12.3%.

Re-development in the centre

Rebuilding in the central business district and the surrounding areas of the inner city has been very important since the 1960s when the Bull Ring was opened (1963). Figure B shows the re-development to the west of the CBD around the National Indoor Arena. Figure C gives details of the Millenium Point project which is situated to the east of the CBD.

Using census statistics

Two useful indicators of wealth in Birmingham are mapped in Figures D and E. A pattern can be detected with less wealthy central areas and more affluence in the outer wards. Figure F is a **relationship graph** drawn to show the two indicators: percentage of households with no car and percentage unemployed. There is a **positive relationship** in this case.

Figure G shows the relationship of another variable with the percentage unemployed and again the relationship is positive. In this case the graph shows that the areas which have a high percentage of Indian, Pakistani or Bangladeshi residents are also areas of high unemployment. The wards with low levels of unemployment tend to have lower percentages of non-white residents.

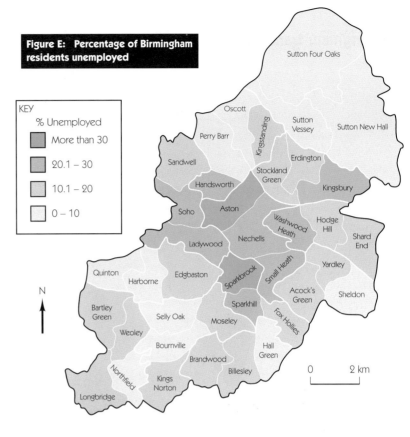

Figure E: Percentage of Birmingham residents unemployed

KEY
% Unemployed
- More than 30
- 20.1 – 30
- 10.1 – 20
- 0 – 10

0   2 km

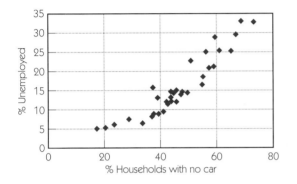

Figure F: Scattergraph showing the relationship between percentage households without a car and percentage unemployed

Figure G: Scattergraph showing the relationship between percentage of residents in the Indian/ Pakistani/ Bangladeshi Ethnic Group and the percentage unemployed

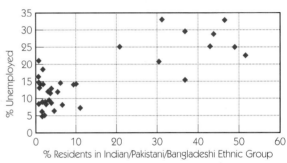

Figure D: Percentage of Birmingham households by Ward without a car

KEY
% households without a car
- More than 60
- 45.1 – 60
- 30.1 – 45
- 0 – 30

0   2 km

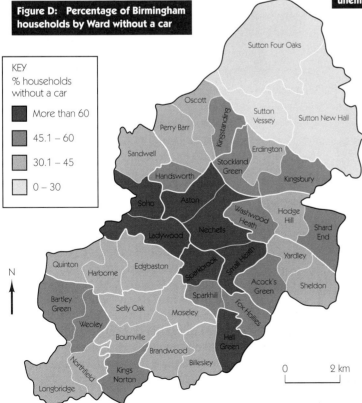

▼ Questions

1 Study the photograph of the National Indoor Arena (Figure B).
  a   Describe the land uses.
  b   State how such re-development will help to regenerate this inner area of Birmingham.

2 Where is the Millennium Point development (Figure C)? What will be built here? What will the benefits be?

3 In what ways do you think transport needs to be improved in the city centre in order make new developments like the National Indoor Arena accessible to all?

4 Describe and explain the patterns shown on the map of percentage of households without a car.

5 In what ways are the patterns of percentage unemployed similar to the patterns of percentage households without a car?

6 Describe and explain the two relationship graphs (Figures F and G).

7 Suggest other indicators which could be used to show the areas of wealth and poverty in Birmingham.

Birmingham: transect along the Coventry Road

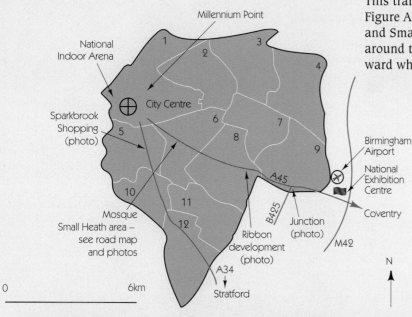

This transect follows the line of the A45 Coventry Road (see Figure A and I). It starts in the inner city wards of Sparkbrook and Small Heath and passes through a new development around the Small Heath Business Park. It ends in Sheldon ward which borders Birmingham Airport in Solihull.

KEY to Wards

1	Nechells	7	Yardley
2	Washwood Heath	8	Acock's Green
3	Hodge Hill	9	Sheldon
4	Shard End	10	Sparkhill
5	Sparkbrook	11	Fox Hollies
6	Small Heath	12	Hall Green

Figure A: The location of the wards of south east Birmingham and the transect along the A45 Coventry Road

Figure D: The Sikh Temple at Small Heath

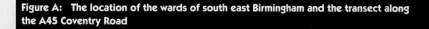

Figure B: Sparkbrook shopping street

Figure C: Terraced housing in Byron Road

Figure E: The Mosque at Poets Corner on the Coventry Road

Sparkbrook is the most overcrowded ward in Birmingham (based on the indicator 'households with over 1.0 persons per room'). It has the highest percentage of unemployment. 46% of its residents are in the Indian/Pakistani/Bangladeshi ethnic group and 13% are in the Black (African/Caribbean) ethnic group. Only 11% of households are owner occupiers. It is an area of **inner city deprivation**. Its shopping streets are lively, colourful and contain a wide cultural variety of shops and services. There are many old terraced houses but there are also small modern houses at lower densities.

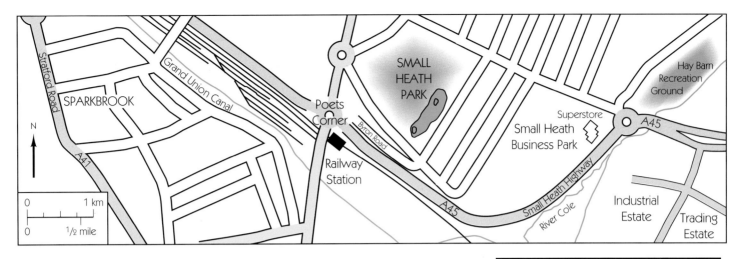

Figure I: Map of Sparkbrook and Small Heath

Figure F: Small Heath Business Park, Talbot Way

Figure H: Ribbon development along the Coventry Road

Figure G: The A45/B425 Junction

Sheldon is one of the least overcrowded wards in Birmingham. Its low percentage unemployment makes it rank 30th out of the 39 wards. It is a fairly affluent area on the edge of Birmingham, with 97% white residents and 32% owner occupying households. Houses are more modern than the inner city. At the eastern end there is a golf course and the Sheldon Country Park.

▼ Questions

1 Describe the scene in each photograph (Figures B to H), giving details about the type of housing, functions of buildings and the urban environment.

2 a What evidence is there of re-development in the Small Heath area?

 b What evidence is there that the eastern end of the transect is more modern?

3 Draw a simple sketch map from the road map (Figure I). Use colours to label the A45, a canal, a river, a park, a Business Park, a superstore and railway land.

4 a Using statistical evidence describe the social and cultural differences of Sparkbrook and Sheldon wards. ➡

 b What reasons can you give for the contrasts between these two wards? ➡

Birmingham: NEC and airport

The area shown on the 1:50,000 Ordnance Survey map (Figure A) is to the east of the transect along the A45 which is the A road running west/east across the map. Study the OS map alongside the plan of the National Exhibition Centre (Figure D).

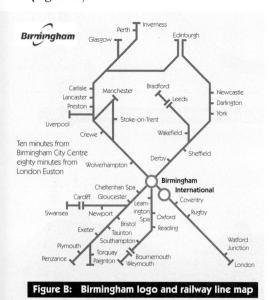

Figure B: Birmingham logo and railway line map

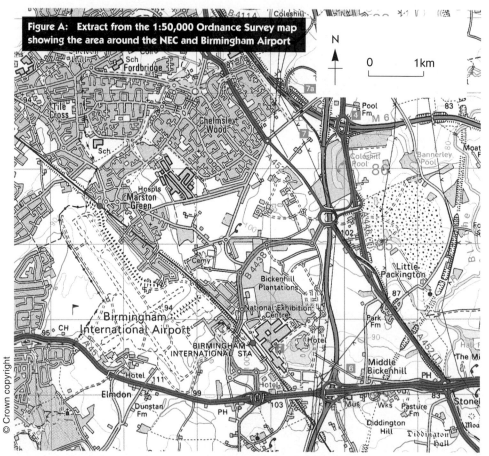

Figure A: Extract from the 1:50,000 Ordnance Survey map showing the area around the NEC and Birmingham Airport

0   1km

N

© Crown copyright

The National Exhibition Centre

The NEC was opened in 1976 and has become a focus for national exhibitions, conventions and concerts. It has hosted the Motor Show, the Motor Cycle Show and the BBC Clothes Show Live.

Over four million people visit the NEC each year. The NEC Arena seats 12,300 spectators. There are several halls that are used for specialised exhibitions. The floor space is more than double that of London's major exhibition centres e.g. Earl's Court, Olympia and Wembley. Transport in the area has been improved to accommodate the large numbers of visitors. There is parking for 18,000 cars. Birmingham International Airport has helped its development. It is located at the centre of Britain's motorway network and is on a mainline railway route from London.

Birmingham International Airport

After the growth of package holidays and general air travel in the 1970s a new terminal was opened at Birmingham Airport in 1984. In 1991 the new 200 bed Eurohub Hotel was opened. In 1996 Birmingham International Airport submitted a **planning application** to Solihull Council outlining an extension to passenger terminals and for a new access and exit slip road to the A45 (Figure E). There was no proposal to extend a runway. These proposals will double the number of passengers to about 10 million by 2005/6.

During 1996 there was a series of public meetings. The airport and Solihull Council set out to answer the questions of nearby residents.

Will air quality be checked?
Complaints will be dealt with by a Hotline.

Will noise insulation grants continue?
Yes. The airport has also agreed to look at a number of schools in the area.

What is going to happen to aircraft noise?
By 2002 older noisier aircraft will have been replaced by quieter aircraft.

What is being done to increase public transport use by passengers and employees?
The aim is to increase the use of public transport from 12% to 20% by 2005/6

What about night flying?
There will be a minimum of night flights and the Council is trying to ban them altogether

What will the airport give back to the community?
The Airport has agreed to plant trees and provide a play area in the areas affected by noise.

Figure C: Views on the airport proposals

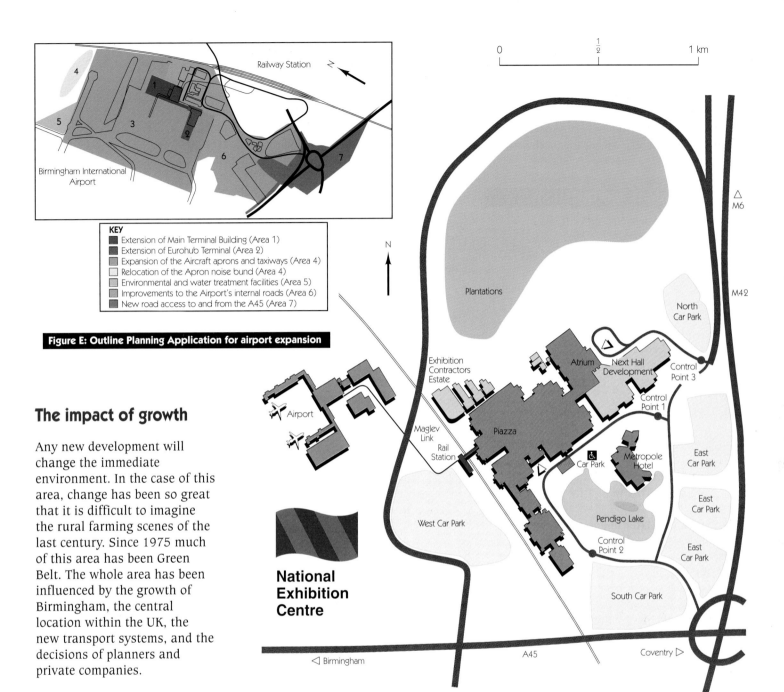

KEY

- Extension of Main Terminal Building (Area 1)
- Extension of Eurohub Terminal (Area 2)
- Expansion of the Aircraft aprons and taxiways (Area 4)
- Relocation of the Apron noise bund (Area 4)
- Environmental and water treatment facilities (Area 5)
- Improvements to the Airport's internal roads (Area 6)
- New road access to and from the A45 (Area 7)

Figure E: Outline Planning Application for airport expansion

The impact of growth

Any new development will change the immediate environment. In the case of this area, change has been so great that it is difficult to imagine the rural farming scenes of the last century. Since 1975 much of this area has been Green Belt. The whole area has been influenced by the growth of Birmingham, the central location within the UK, the new transport systems, and the decisions of planners and private companies.

National Exhibition Centre

Figure D: The National Exhibition Centre

▼ Questions

1. Draw a sketch map of the area shown on the OS map extract (Figure A) to show land use. Label the NEC, Birmingham Airport, housing, a hospital, a golf course, business development and lines of transport. Label the golf course and the area to the east of motorway M42 Green Belt.
2. Design your own spray diagram to show the site details of the NEC.
3. Why do you think the NEC has become the focus for national and international events?
4. List the evidence for the growth of settlement in the area covered by the Ordnance Survey map (Figure A).
5. Choose three separate developments you listed and discuss their possible impact on the surrounding environment. ➡
6. In what ways might the proposed expansion of Birmingham Airport affect the local population:
   a in terms of disruption
   b in terms of benefits? ➡

Review

Census information can be used to analyse social and cultural characteristics of cities. Birmingham, like other cities, has been re-developed in the central area and has grown outwards towards the countryside. The area around the NEC is an example of planned urban development in a former rural area.

CASE STUDY: Sheffield – revitalising a city

Main activity

In this exercise the main tasks are report writing, data response questions and dealing with issues.

Key ideas and questions

● Sheffield has been transformed from an industrial city to a modern regional centre.
● Its employment, land use, transport and landscapes have changed.
● Funding for change has come from government and European sources.
● Why did Sheffield's reputation for steel grow and decline?
● How do the new jobs differ from the old?
● How will the Supertram help revitalise the city?
● What are the characteristics of the Meadowhall Shopping Centre?

Sheffield in South Yorkshire is one of Britain's largest cities; since the fourteenth century it has built up a reputation for making high quality knives and tools. This industrial growth was based on:

1 local iron ore (later imported)
2 forests providing the wood for charcoal (also imported)
3 fast-flowing streams to operate waterwheels
4 millstone grit from which grinding stones were made
5 limestone for iron making from the Pennines
6 gannister, a local clay, for fire-bricks to line the furnaces
7 the invention in 1742 of 'Sheffield plate': a steel alloy with a copper and silver coating (from 1850 electro-plating was used)
8 local coal (from the time of Industrial Revolution)
9 the development of the Sheffield and Tinsley Canal in 1819
10 the development of a railway to Rotherham in 1838 and later roads.

The Lower Don valley

Sheffield's steel industry spread down the Don valley (Figure A). Steel castings, railway carriages, and heavy steel goods were produced. At its peak there were 40,000 jobs but 23,000 of

these were lost in just five years in the 1980s. One-third of the land in the Don valley was left derelict after terraced slum housing and steel works had been cleared. In 1988 the government set up the Sheffield Development Corporation to revitalise the valley and generate new employment. Money was attracted from private sources as well as government and European grants and loans. The Development Corporation was not as large as that in London Docklands and it only lasted nine years until 1997. The map (Figure B) shows the main characteristics of the new valley.

The Lower Don valley is no longer dominated by steel manufacturing. Today there are over 900 businesses employing 24,000 people; this includes the 7000 employees in the Meadowhall Shopping complex. Distribution industries now account for 50% of the businesses in the valley. Other expanding areas of employment are transport, leisure and financial services. Figures C and D show the Atlas North industrial site before and after re-development. When the land at Atlas North was derelict the issue was 'What should be done with the land?' Re-development resolved this issue and Atlas North has become a part of the new Don Valley.

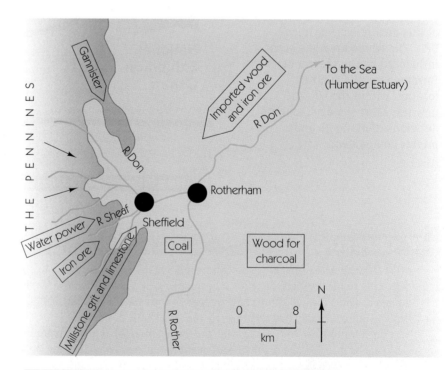

Figure A: The factors leading to the industrial growth of Sheffield

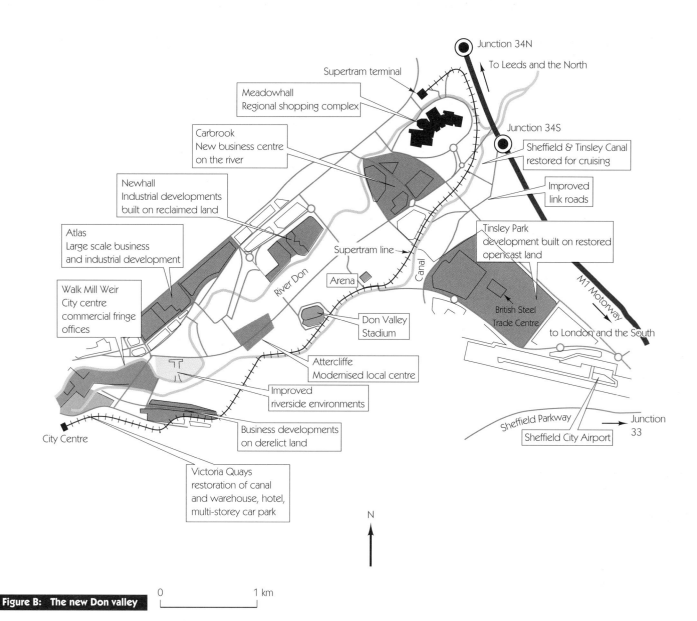

Junction 34N
To Leeds and the North

Supertram terminal

Meadowhall
Regional shopping complex

Carbrook
New business centre
on the river

Junction 34S

Sheffield & Tinsley Canal
restored for cruising

Newhall
Industrial developments
built on reclaimed land

Improved
link roads

Atlas
Large scale business
and industrial development

Tinsley Park
development built on restored
opencast land

Supertram line

Canal

Arena

River Don

Walk Mill Weir
City centre
commercial fringe
offices

British Steel
Trade Centre

M1 Motorway

Don Valley
Stadium

to London and the South

Attercliffe
Modernised local centre

Improved
riverside environments

City Centre

Business developments
on derelict land

Sheffield Parkway

Junction
33

Sheffield City Airport

Victoria Quays
restoration of canal
and warehouse, hotel,
multi-storey car park

N

0   1 km

Figure B: The new Don valley

Figure C: Atlas North, before re-development

Figure D: Atlas North, after the re-development

Figure E shows a part of the Don valley in the 1930s. The changes along the valley from heavy metal industry to multiple uses has raised issues for many local people.

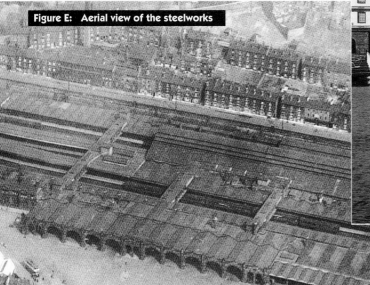

Figure E: Aerial view of the steelworks

Figure F: Victoria Quays

Figure G: Abbey National Headquarters

Costs and benefits of development

- Does the Victoria Quays (Figure F) re-development benefit local residents?
- Is the employment offered at the Abbey National Headquarters (Figure G) relevant to the local residents?
- Are the benefits of the Supertram (Figures H and I) going to outweigh the massive costs?
- Has the opening of the Meadowhall shopping centre (Figure J) damaged local shopping?

Each one of these issues can be understood and analysed by asking a series of questions.

- What is the issue?
- Who is involved?
- What are the important features of this issue?
- Why are they like this?
- How might this issue be resolved?
- What might be the consequences for different groups of people?
- What do you think should happen and why?

The Sheffield Supertram

The Supertram is a **light rail system** which cost £250 million. Since 1994 it has run along three main lines linking many of Sheffield's main attractions (Figure I). The busiest line is the one along the Lower Don valley to Meadowhall. Other modern light rail systems in Britain include Manchester Metrolink, Tyne and Wear Metro, Blackpool trams and the London Docklands Light Railway.

Figure H: The Supertram

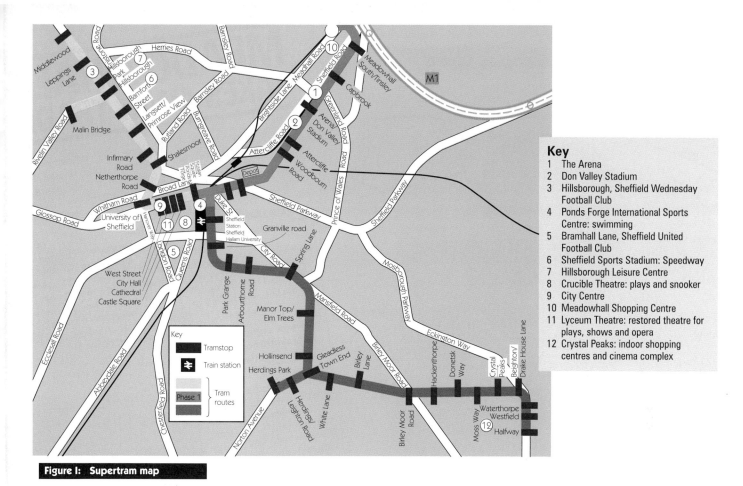

Figure I: Supertram map

Key
1. The Arena
2. Don Valley Stadium
3. Hillsborough, Sheffield Wednesday Football Club
4. Ponds Forge International Sports Centre: swimming
5. Bramhall Lane, Sheffield United Football Club
6. Sheffield Sports Stadium: Speedway
7. Hillsborough Leisure Centre
8. Crucible Theatre: plays and snooker
9. City Centre
10. Meadowhall Shopping Centre
11. Lyceum Theatre: restored theatre for plays, shows and opera
12. Crystal Peaks: indoor shopping centres and cinema complex

The advantages of the Supertram

- clean – no exhaust fumes
- no car parking problems
- Supertram can carry as many people as 160 cars
- helps to prevent future growth in road congestion
- quiet and comfortable travel
- low floor single decker – no stairs
- reliable service: every 10 or 15 minutes except on the line south (every 30 minutes)
- can travel up to 50 mph
- funded by the government and some from European Regional Development Fund (ERDF)
- continues to run in bad weather including snow
- links major sports and leisure centres with the city centre
- children travel to school on it
- a very good safety record despite the lines running in the roads: the Supertram should reduce accident costs in the city
- environmental improvements including tree planting along some routes
- provided employment during the building phases
- provides employment in its operating processes
- Some of the benefits of the Supertram are for **non-users**, e.g. environmental improvements, reduction in accident costs and reducing road congestion. These can be referred to as **external benefits**.

Do you know?

? The reasons for the decline of Sheffield's steel industry were similar to the reasons for de-industrialisation in other heavy industrial areas.

? Low cost **foreign imports** of steel goods.

? **Mechanisation** and automation of processes.

? **Inefficient methods** and high labour costs compared to new producing countries.

? **New materials** such as plastics being used instead of steel.

▼ Questions

1. Write a report on The Lower Don valley using the following sub-headings:
   - Sheffield's Industrial Past
   - The Steel Industry Declines
   - New Development in the Lower Don valley
   - The Supertram helps to revitalise the city ➡

2. How do you think the following Sheffield people feel about the new Lower Don valley?
   - The steel worker who lost his job in the valley in 1985
   - The family who lost their home in the valley when it was demolished
   - The businesswoman who is looking for a new office unit
   - The school children who live locally

3. Choose one of the issues mentioned in this section. Plan an enquiry to follow through the chosen issue. What other questions do you want to ask? ➡

Sheffield: The Meadowhall Shopping Centre

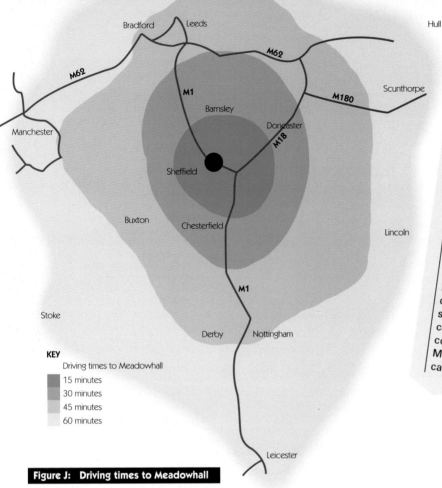

KEY

Driving times to Meadowhall

- 15 minutes
- 30 minutes
- 45 minutes
- 60 minutes

Figure J: Driving times to Meadowhall

Figure K: Meadowhall shopper profile

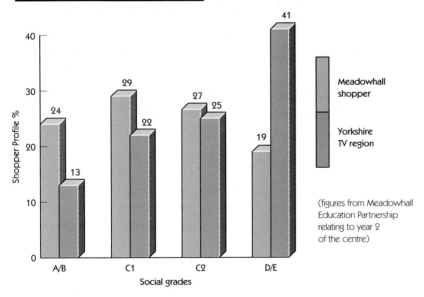

(figures from Meadowhall Education Partnership relating to year 2 of the centre)

Key: Social grades or classes used by the Registrar General

A Upper professional/manager/administrative
B Lower professional/manager/executive
C1 supervisory/clerical
C2 skilled workers
D semi-skilled workers
E unskilled workers

MEADOWHALL TAKES AWAY TRADE

A market research company has found that there has been some movement of trade away from Sheffield City Centre. In 1992 the average decline was 16%. 71% of traders thought their turnover had decreased. There was of course a recession which accounted for some of the decline, but not all of it.

Service outlets in the city centre appear to be least affected.

Not only has the city centre suffered. Many small neighbourhood centres have also felt the competition from Meadowhall. 'My books can tell you the exact week Meadowhall opened', one retailer in the south of Sheffield told a customer the week before he closed down his shop.

The impact of Meadowhall was also felt forty kilometres to the south of Sheffield at Matlock. In the small town centre the Marks and Spencer store closed in the same week that Meadowhall opened!

Figure L

Until the 1960s new shopping developments in the UK were sited in existing centres. Then food supermarkets began to move to the outskirts of towns. Later DIY centres, carpet and furniture shops moved to **out-of-town** locations. In 1976 the first regional shopping centre opened at Brent Cross in North London. Two of the largest regional shopping centres are the Metro Centre in Gateshead and the Meadowhall Centre in Sheffield. Meadowhall is at the top of the regional shopping hierarchy with both **convenience** and **comparison goods** for sale. The **threshold population** for the centre is high: about 9 million people live within one hour's drive. People are willing to travel long distances to Meadowhall to buy certain goods.

Do you know?

? **Low order** or **convenience** goods e.g. food
? **High order** or **comparison goods**: shoes, furniture
? There is a **shopping hierarchy** or pyramid pattern structure of shopping centres
? **Threshold population:** the minimum number of customers a business needs in order to make a profit
? **Range** of a good: the distance people are willing to travel to purchase a product

Meadowhall Shopping Centre

Location

- Within the Lower Don valley redevelopment area

Site

- Large area of flat land. On land once occupied by Hadfield Steel Works which closed in 1983

Access

- Accessible from M1 Motorway Junction 34
- 12,000 free car parking spaces
- Two new rail stations
- Bus station on site
- Supertram to be built linking the city centre
- Most people travel by car but an impressive 24% use public transport. 49% travel more than 10 miles.

Employment

- 7000 people (full and part time)
- The average shopper is 'upmarket' compared to the population of the local commercial TV region

Layout

- Over 270 shops and restaurants based on six themed shopping malls eg. Oasis, The Coca-Cola Arcade (private companies have sponsored the theme areas such as the Ty-Phoo Tots Creche)
- There are 7 major stores which are called 'anchor' stores and have a focal point for the areas e.g. Sainsbury's Savacentre and Marks and Spencer, House of Fraser and Debenhams

Surrounding developments

- Multiplex cinema
- Nearby retail warehouse park including Toys Я Us and MFI
- Don Valley Stadium
- Sheffield Arena
- Carbrook Hall Office Park including Abbey National Building Society
- Leisure theme park on former derelict land

It's not all perfect

The newspaper article (Figure L) states that shops around Sheffield felt the impact of Meadowhall when it opened. As people visited Meadowhall so the small shops and local shopping centres made less profit. Meadowhall has particularly attracted the more prosperous, or 'upmarket' shopper. There seems to be less benefit to people in social class D and E who comprise 41% of the region's population.

Other disadvantages of Meadowhall

- For many it is expensive to travel there
- It takes time to travel there
- It does not have shops selling cheap goods
- Rents are high and small shops cannot afford them

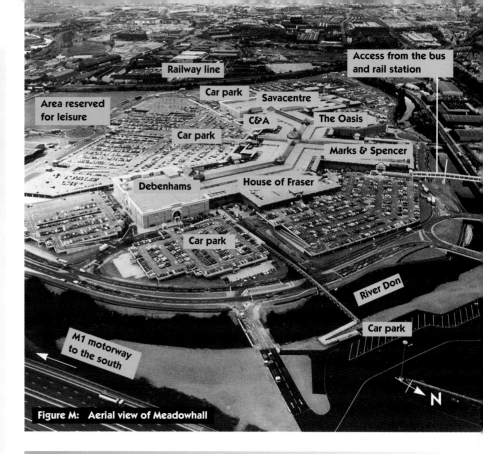

Figure M: Aerial view of Meadowhall

▼ Questions

1. a Where is the Meadowhall regional shopping centre located?
   b What were the advantages of the Meadowhall site?
2. a What is the threshold population of Meadowhall?
   b Some goods on sale at Meadowhall have a high range. What is meant by this?
   c Why would you say Meadowhall is at the top of the regional shopping hierarchy?
3. a In what ways is the centre accessible for customers using private and public transport?
   b Why is it important for the centre to have anchor stores?
4. In a small group discuss some of the advantages and disadvantages of the Meadowhall shopping centre. Approach the discussion from different people's viewpoints.

Extension question

5. Neighbourhood Shopping Centre or Regional Shopping centre?
   This is the question many local people would like to discuss. Unfortunately the local people do not usually have a say in the decision making. The decisions are taken by local authorities, development corporations and private companies.
   Consider the points of view of people from social grades C2, D and E living 10 miles (16 kilometres) from a proposed new regional shopping centre. What will they think of the regional shopping centre proposals? Would they prefer a revitalised neighbourhood shopping centre in their own housing area? The arguments can be written in the form of bubble diagrams.

Review

Sheffield has been transformed from a steel city to one offering a wide range of employment which should be sustained. The Lower Don valley with the Meadowhall Shopping complex is the centre of the revitalisation process.

5 Northern Ireland: life in a peripheral region

Northern Ireland (Figure A) is a **peripheral region** because it is a long way from the core of the UK and Europe. It is a region of low agricultural productivity and has had a declining industrial base. It has social and economic characteristics which explain why it lags behind the rest of the UK (Figure B). Its main city is Belfast, which has inner city problems similar to those experienced all over Europe. The country has suffered with the 'Troubles' since 1969 during which period over 3100 people have been killed. It is not a region that is now in decline as it is attracting inward investment. It would be best described as a

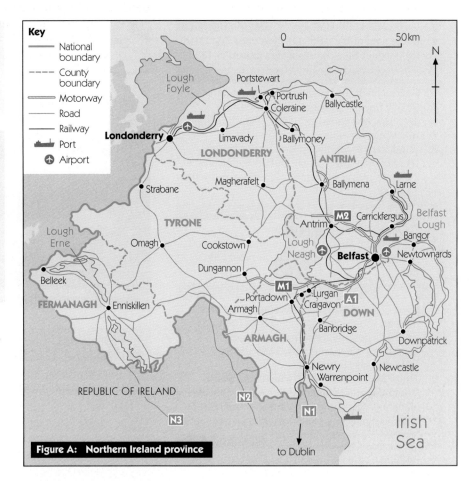

Figure A: Northern Ireland province

changing peripheral region where the prospects could be very favourable. But political peace is probably necessary to secure a sustainable economic future.

Economic characteristics

● Lower weekly wage rates than in the UK as a whole
● Unemployment rates 50% higher than the UK average
● Commercial rents less than 50% of the UK average
● Low land and property prices
● High transport costs to mainland UK and Europe
● Low traffic densities
● Poorly developed tourist sector

Social characteristics

● Highest birth rate in the UK and Europe
● Youngest age structure in the UK (25% under age 15 years)
● Net emigration (especially to the USA) and net out-migration to other parts of the UK
● Rural de-population and the decline of rural communities
● The highest proportion of household income coming from social security payments in the UK
● Low rate of car ownership
● GCSE and A Level pass rates are higher than the UK as a whole
● Highest rate of 16 year olds in full time education in the UK

Figure B: The characteristics that define Northern Ireland as a peripheral region

The attractive economy

Many of the social and economic characteristics shown in Figure B indicate a poor region. But they also are the reason for the attractiveness of Northern Ireland to the inward investor. The Industrial Development Board for Northern Ireland co-ordinates industrial investment and many foreign and British companies have set up in the region. The economy of the region is being re-structured. Figure C shows how the region can be made to appear very attractive. The new **inward investment** has changed the economy from one that could have gone into a **spiral of decline** to one that is already in a **cycle of wealth** (cycle of growth).

Some industrial investment examples of inward investment include:

- Du Pont (USA): synthetic rubber and man-made fibres, Londonderry
- Fruit of the Loom: cotton and textile products, Londonderry
- Fujitsu (Japan): telecommunications, Antrim
- Daewoo (Korea): electronic tuners, Carrickfergus; and video cassette recorders, Antrim
- Montupet (France): aluminium castings (car components), Belfast

The links between Northern Ireland and the Republic of Ireland are improving. There are EU grants for cross-border co-operation (the INTEREG programme). Of all Ireland's population, 50% live in the 20% of land between Belfast and Dublin (Figure A). This is a axis of economic growth (called the Emerald Corridor) which could develop if there is a lasting peace. The ports of Larne and Dun Laoghaire serve the Emerald Corridor. Tourism could increase in this area once tourists can move between the north and south more easily. Some companies already operate either side of the border. Fruit of the Loom supply the British and European markets from factories both sides of the border using the port of Larne.

▼ Questions

1. What is a peripheral region?
2. Why does Northern Ireland lag behind the UK as a whole? Choose six reasons from Figure B to answer this.
3. Study Figure C. In what ways are the attractions of Northern Ireland similar to the problems shown in Figure B?
4. Give some examples of inward investment into Northern Ireland.

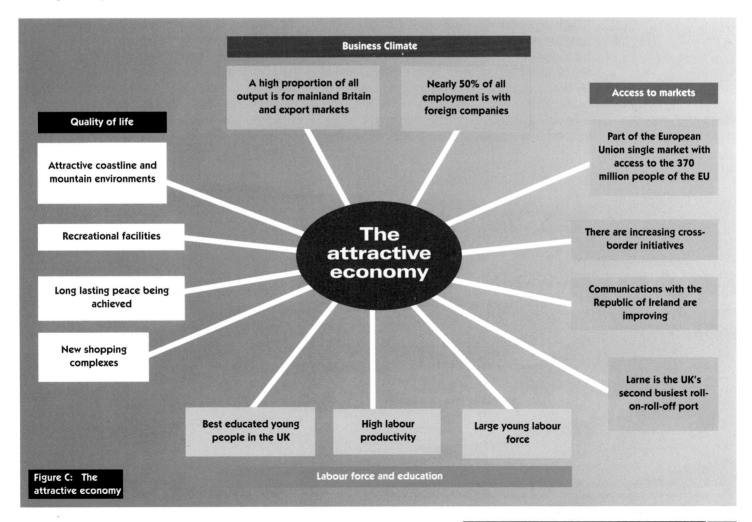

Figure C: The attractive economy

▼ Questions

5 Why has a possible spiral of decline been stopped in Northern Ireland? (Refer to page 54.)

6 This is an enquiry exercise and could be done as group work.

The question is, 'Why invest in manufacturing industry in Northern Ireland?'

a You will find the information on the Northern Ireland pages, 90–93.

b You can present your findings in a variety of ways, e.g. graphs, maps, bubble diagrams, spray diagrams or lists.

c Summarise what your findings tell you.

d What is the answer to the question?

e End by stating what other information you need and how you could have improved your exercise.

Capital
● Cash grants for buildings and machinery up to 50%

Revenue
● Grants towards start up costs
● Grants to reduce interest payments on loans
● Factory rent grants up to 100% of factory rents for 5 years
● Support for Research and Development programmes

Tax
● Reduced tax payments

Finance
● Providing loans including interest-free periods

European funding
● Is available under the European Regional Development Fund. Northern Ireland is an Objective 1 region and receives EU Structural funds

Figure D: Some of the financial incentives offered in Northern Ireland. Similar grants are available in other UK regions.

Rural development

For many years in Northern Ireland there has been a **drift** away from the land resulting in **rural depopulation**. It is usually the younger people who leave the rural areas where there is a high dependence on farming, a lack of industry and poorly developed services and infrastructure.

The Rural Development Programme started in 1991 and encourages people to stay in the countryside. Grants are used to stimulate economic activity. In a similar way to the industrial development grants, there are grants for farming, leisure and the tourist industry. Funds come from the British government as well as the EU. By the mid-1990s the Rural Development Programme had been involved with 450 community organisations and 42 local projects; some 375 jobs had received support. Figure F shows some features of the programme up to 2000.

Figure E: A fishing village assisted by the Rural Development Programme

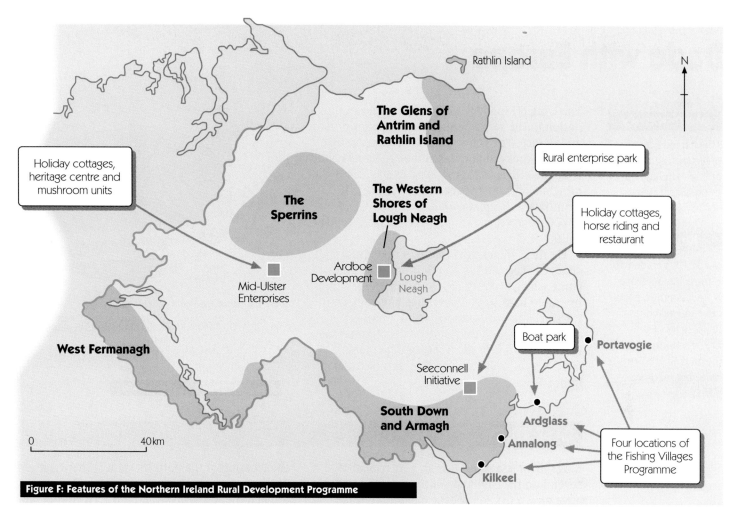

Figure F: Features of the Northern Ireland Rural Development Programme

Map labels:
- Rathlin Island
- N
- The Glens of Antrim and Rathlin Island
- Holiday cottages, heritage centre and mushroom units
- The Sperrins
- The Western Shores of Lough Neagh
- Rural enterprise park
- Holiday cottages, horse riding and restaurant
- Ardboe Development
- Lough Neagh
- Mid-Ulster Enterprises
- West Fermanagh
- Boat park
- Portavogie
- Seeconnell Initiative
- South Down and Armagh
- Ardglass
- Annalong
- Four locations of the Fishing Villages Programme
- Kilkeel
- 0   40km

Grants do not always benefit everybody in an area. Critics say that they can cause jobs to be moved around from place to place, known as **job displacement**. Many grants are used for **job creation** when it is said they could be used to support people already in jobs. There have been examples where a grant to a new business causes the failure of an existing one. There is a major problem with grants to leisure and tourism. These sectors of the economy are **seasonal** and what is earned in the summer has to subsidise the rest of the year.

Figure G: The Rural Development Programme focuses on disadvantaged areas

▼ Questions

1 What is meant by:
  a the drift from the land
  b rural depopulation
  c a high dependence on farming?
2 What has the Rural Development Programme set out to do?
3 What are the sources of funding for the Programme?
4 What do you think is meant by a rural disadvantaged area?
5 Why are fishing villages receiving financial assistance?
6 Which activities receiving rural aid are mainly seasonal businesses?
7 Discuss the advantages and disadvantages of giving a grant to one holiday cottage enterprise. (Think about the ways the grant will lead to local employment and how it could lead to job displacement.)

Review

Inward investment into Northern Ireland has halted a spiral of decline. Both urban and rural areas receive grants to help diversify the economy. Grants can cause job displacement as well as job creation.

Trade with Europe

Main activity

This exercise involves investigating the sale of East Anglian wheat to Russia.

Key ideas

● The UK's trade with Europe has increased.
● East Anglian ports have increased in importance. They have modernised and introduced efficient handling methods.

The United Kingdom is the fifth largest trading nation in the world behind USA, Japan, Germany and France. The country needs to **export** some goods in order to purchase other goods which it is not so efficient at producing itself. This is the principle of trade between nations. The UK manufactures aircraft for export in order to import goods it cannot produce such as tropical fruits.

Figure A shows how the UK's trade has changed. The UK has a **deficit** on its **balance of trade** which is offset by a **surplus** on its **invisible balance**. Oil revenues have helped the UK since the 1970s, contributing to 6% of exports. Although the UK depends on imports of raw materials and some food products these make up a smaller and smaller part of total **import** costs.

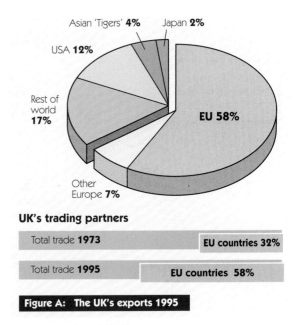

Asian 'Tigers' **4%**   Japan **2%**
USA **12%**
Rest of world **17%**
EU **58%**
Other Europe **7%**

UK's trading partners

Total trade **1973**	**EU countries 32%**
Total trade **1995**	**EU countries 58%**

Figure A: The UK's exports 1995

CASE STUDY: The port of Kings Lynn

Kings Lynn is a small British port typical of several on the east and south east coasts that have grown to cater for the expanding trade with Europe. The Bentinck Dock was built over 100 years ago and handles grain, petroleum products and timber (Figure B). In the 1990s new mechanical equipment was introduced and a new 220-metre riverside quay was opened. This allows ships of 5,000 dwt to use the port (Figure C). This ship will take about five days to reach Russia from Kings Lynn. Figure D shows the location of the port, its trade, other East Anglian ports and communications. The roads are being improved throughout East Anglia, and Kings Lynn is becoming more accessible. A detailed breakdown of Kings Lynn's trade is shown in Figure E.

Figure B: Timber exports

METSÄ TIMBER   METSÄ TIMBER
ETSÄ TIMBER   METSÄ TIMBER
KL8-3
TSÄ TIMBER   METSÄ TIMBER

Figure C: Grain exports

Do you know?

? The language of trade
? Trade in goods is **visible trade**
? The difference in value between exports and imports of goods is the **balance of trade**. This may be a **surplus** or **deficit**
? The buying and selling of services such as banking, insurance and tourism is **invisible trade**
? The combination of visible and invisible trade is the **balance of payments**

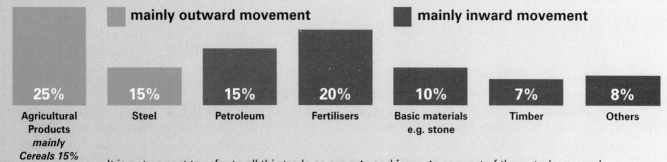

mainly outward movement				mainly inward movement		
25%	15%	15%	20%	10%	7%	8%
Agricultural Products *mainly Cereals 15% and animal feedstuffs 10%*	Steel	Petroleum	Fertilisers	Basic materials e.g. stone	Timber	Others

It is not correct to refer to all this trade as **exports** and **imports** as most of the petroleum and basic materials is UK coastal trade involving small vessels moving between UK ports.

Figure E: Kings Lynn trade

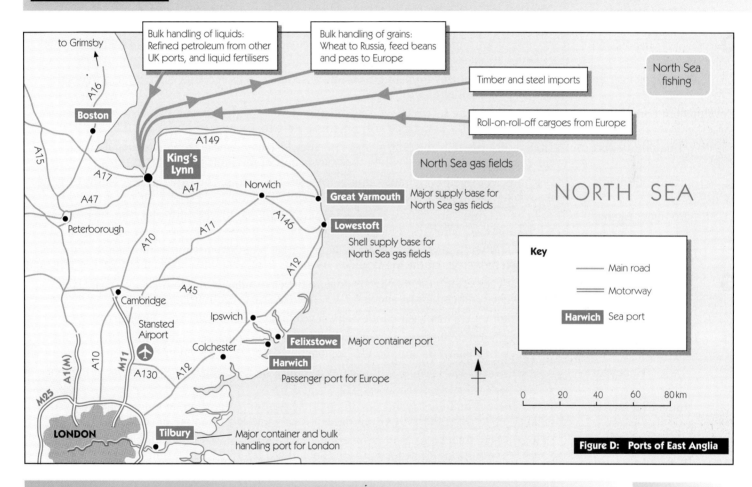

Bulk handling of liquids: Refined petroleum from other UK ports, and liquid fertilisers

Bulk handling of grains: Wheat to Russia, feed beans and peas to Europe

Timber and steel imports

Roll-on-roll-off cargoes from Europe

North Sea fishing

to Grimsby

Boston

North Sea gas fields

King's Lynn

Norwich

Great Yarmouth Major supply base for North Sea gas fields

NORTH SEA

Peterborough

Lowestoft

Shell supply base for North Sea gas fields

Key
—— Main road
═══ Motorway
Harwich Sea port

Cambridge

Stansted Airport

Ipswich

Colchester

Felixstowe Major container port

Harwich

Passenger port for Europe

N

0 20 40 60 80 km

LONDON

Tilbury Major container and bulk handling port for London

Figure D: Ports of East Anglia

▼ Questions

1. Write a description of the UK's current trade situation.
2. Name some products Britain can not produce itself. How can the country earn money to pay for these imports?
3. In what ways has Kings Lynn expanded to increase its trade?
4. a You are a part of a British trade mission in Moscow. Your job is to sell surplus wheat from East Anglian farms to Russia where harvests have been poor. You are required to design a leaflet to convince the Russians that they need to buy wheat from Britain.

Include a description of the wheat growing areas of East Anglia.
List the ways the wheat would be transported from the farms to Russia.
Draw a map of the route the wheat would take from East Anglia to St. Petersburg.

b Argue the case for selling wheat to the Russians to a group of East Anglian school children who say the wheat should be kept to eat in the UK. They need to be introduced to the principles and language of trade.

B Beach replenishment — Building up a beach by feeding it with material from off-shore or by road trucks, as at Seaford and as at Eastbourne in 1997–98, *16–19*

Brownfield site — A site which has been developed and is available for re-development and new building, e.g. South Marston Park and Honda in Swindon, *60*, and the Millennium Dome site, *74–75*

C Capital intensive — Industry which uses a high proportion of money, buildings and equipment, as opposed to one which employs a lot of people which is referred to as labour intensive, *34–37*

Costs and benefits — A way of evaluating developments by looking at what has been gained (benefit) and what has been lost (cost). These do not have to be in solely financial terms, e.g. there can be environmental and social costs and benefits, *28, 31*, South Wales, *66–67*

Cumulative Causation — Where new investment leads to growth and more investment. The process of Myrdal's growth model and the multiplier effect, *54–55*, e.g. M4 Corridor, *58–61*

D Depression — An area of low pressure where the winds circulate anti-clockwise and fronts separate different air masses. Depressions move into the British Isles from the Atlantic, *12–15*

Development Area — An area receiving government grants and assistance to promote its economy, e.g. Teesside, *34–37*, South Wales, *62–67*

Development Corporation — A organising body set up to oversee and plan development in a small area such as Teesside, *34–37*, London Docklands, *74–77*, Sheffield, *84–89*

Doughnut effect — The process whereby the central areas of cities lose population as industries and business close down and move out. 'Filling the hole' is part of re-vitalising the city centres

E Effluents — Discharges of waste water and outfalls from sewage works. They are not necessarily dirty as they have come from processing plants, *16–19*

Environment Agency — The organisation that took over the work of the National Rivers Authority. The Agency looks after water environments in England and Wales, *26–27*

F Footloose industry — An industry with no strong raw material or market requirements for its location, e.g. the high-tech industries of the M4 Corridor, *58–61*

G Green tourism — Tourism where minimum damage is done to the environment and tourists experience the natural environment, e.g. Exmoor, *40–45*. Referred to as eco-tourism

Greenfield site — A site where there has been no previous development, e.g. Slade Farm, Bicester, *70–73*

H High-tech industry — The description of industry using high technology and computer aided equipment, e.g. Intel European Headquarters and the EMI compact disc factory in Swindon

Honeypot — An area which many people visit such as a beauty spot. Blackpool, *38–39*, parts of Exmoor, *40–45*. Referred to as 'tourist magnets'

I Industrial inertia — Where there is an industry but the original reasons for its location no longer apply, e.g. steel making on Teesside the 1990s even though there is no local iron ore or coal, *34–37*

Industrial Park — New offices and factories built in pleasant surroundings on the edge of urban areas, e.g. South Marston Park in Swindon, *56–59*. Sometimes referred to as Business Parks

Infrastructure — The stock of fixed equipment in an area such as roads, railways, gas, water, electricity, tele-communications, drains and sewers, *34–37*

Inner city — The area of the city with old industry and housing, decay and re-development

Inter-tidal mudflats — The areas of wetland exposed between high and low tides which are a habitat for wildlife

Multiplier effect — The spiral of growth which is created by the establishment of a new investment, e.g. a factory. It is the process of cumulative causation in Myrdal's growth model, *54–55*

M
O Organic farming — Farming which depends on natural inputs such as natural fertilisers and operates in a system which does not introduce artificial fertilisers, herbicides and insecticides, *50–53*

R Re-development — Where an area is modernised and re-built. 'Regeneration' and 're-vitalisation' describe the same process, e.g. South Wales and Swansea Bay, *62–67*

S Sustainable development — Development where the resources are conserved over a long period of time, *17–19*

System — A set of inter-related parts, e.g. a drainage basin system which has inputs, processes and outputs and a farm system which can also be seen like this, *26–27, 48–49*

W Wetland — Marshy areas which are a habitat for wildlife, e.g. Poole Harbour, *20–23*